NEW KIDS ON THE BLOCK

THE WHOLE STORY
By Their Friends

Robin McGibbon

Picture by ERIC ANTONIOU

AVON BOOKS NEW YORK

All color tour photos by RETNA

Portraits of New Kids' teachers and friends, and all Dorchester locations by Eric Antoniou

AVON BOOKS
A division of
The Hearst Corporation
105 Madison Avenue
New York, New York 10016

Copyright © 1990 by Robin McGibbon
Front cover photograph by Chris Van Der Vooren
Published by arrangement with the authors
ISBN: 0-380-76344-3

First Avon Books Trade Printing: July 1990

Printed in the U.S.A.

RA   10   9   8   7   6   5   4   3   2   1

FOR RUTH,

*who always said: If you
really want to do something,
go for it.*

PRIZE GUYS: The New Kids and Maurice Starr pick up their first major trophy at the Boston Music Awards in 1989   Picture: ERIC ANTONIOU

MY THANKS

If I had to mention all the kind people of Dorchester who contributed to this book – either the New Kids' friends themselves, or others who didn't know them, but provided phone numbers and addresses of others who did – the list would be as long as the book itself. But there are certain people to whom I owe a great debt, and who must be specially thanked and named; warm, kind people who invited me into their homes and without whom the book, quite simply, would not have been written.

In no particular order, I would like to thank the lovely Linda Crockett, who put me in touch with Joe Gateley at the Hi-Fi pizza, whose memories of Donnie started the ball rolling; Susan Byrne for introducing Karen Finnigan, who traced Jamie Kelley, an original New Kid, whose memories brought the early struggles of the band so much to life; Bertha White, not only for providing personal photographs, but for generously loaning fan magazines and newspaper clippings for research; David Harris and neighbours Liam and John Hughes, for such warm hospitality on a chilly morning; Peter Fitzgerald, whose clarity of recall filled in so many gaps; Michelle McCourt, for vital background on Joey, plus her personal photos; Steve Morse, of the Boston Globe, who responded swiftly, providing much-needed information and welcome refuge on a rainswept night; to Father Oakes for such openness – and for refusing to drop me in the middle of nowhere; Laura Madden for transcribing some of the tape recordings; four young boys – Tommy and Steven Callaghan and their friend Marcos Ercalano in Savin Hill, and Ronnie Padilla in Jamaica Plain, whose contribution is much appreciated even if it didn't make the finished product.

Extra special thanks must go to top Boston photographer Eric Antoniou, for far, far more than just taking pictures; to Sue for all those uncomplaining hours on the manuscript; and to my good pal Jimmy O'Leary, whose artistic mind helped me meet the deadline.

Above all, I would like to thank my father, who knew it could be done and gave me unwavering support when others were sowing seeds of doubt. This positive attitude – plus the odd suggestion – kept me going and, ultimately, helped make my idea a reality.

Robin McGibbon

THE AUTHOR

Robin McGibbon was born in Brockley, South London, in 1965. He went to Bickley Park and Sevenoaks schools in Kent and, after training at journalist college in Cardiff, he started as a reporter on the Wimbledon News. Since 1986 he has been a news reporter and a showbusiness writer for two Fleet Street newspapers. He lives in South London and his mother and three sisters, Katrina, Alison and Jayne, live in Beckenham.

CONTENTS

CONTENTS

1

The Young Entertainer

The New Kids on the Block success story began under the towering trees of a beautiful park on the outskirts of Boston.

It was where Donnie Wahlberg and his friends escaped to when the bus brought them home to Dorchester after school. For them, Dorchester Park was an oasis amid the grimy streets of a tough area, where there was at least one murder and more than 900 muggings every month.

Normally, Donnie and his pals would play basketball and baseball from early afternoon until it was dark and they could barely see the ball. But, that summer of 1984, a new craze had turned them on their heads – a craze that took preference over girls and even the ball-games they loved so much. The new trend was break-dancing and it captivated the kids in that Boston suburb as much as it had the youngsters throughout America – Donnie Wahlberg more than most.

The second youngest child in a family of six, Donnie had always seemed older than his years. He was very self-assured and had a confidence that often bordered on arrogance. To adults who didn't know him well, Donnie would appear cocky, with rather too much to say for himself and a cheeky way of saying it. But to his pals in Dorchester Park he was the kid they all looked up to in some sort of envy, if not awe. He was fiercely independent, with a desire to be different and a charismatic charmer never afraid to speak his mind. He was always first with the latest fashion and organised his friends – just as he had, as a ten-year-old, in the playground of the William Monroe Trotter school in nearby Roxbury.

In short, Donnie Wahlberg was a natural born leader. And, even as a 14-year-old, he revelled in the role.

He was the one who practised longest and hardest at break-dancing, and the one whose agile brain and quick street-wise wit swiftly mastered rapping, the rhyming rage that went with it.

Impressed by his skills, Donnie's pals would beg him to give them a show. He never let them down and basked in the applause his spontaneous raps and dancing brought from his young admirers. Donnie had amazing vision for one so young and he saw the financial potential in break-dancing in public. With equally enthusiastic, if less able, friends, he put on impromptu displays outside stores in downtown Boston on Saturday mornings, earning more than a few dollars from admiring passers-by. To the ambitious Donnie, though, the pocket money was less important than the excitement he felt from performing in front of an audience. He had always loved being the centre of attention, and now, for the first time, he began to believe he might have the talent to become a star. But he was still only fourteen and for the next four years, at least, his life looked like revolving around lessons at the Phyllis Wheatley school and sport with his pals in Dorchester Park.

And then, one afternoon in June, a close friend, Peter Fitzgerald, told him what Gina Marcucci had said.

And Donnie Wahlberg's hope of becoming a star was suddenly more than just a dream.

Peter was the same age as Donnie, but went to a different school, St Ann's, in the Neponset district of Dorchester. He could sing and act and had starred in many of his school's theatrical productions.

One day he was waiting in the park for his pals, when Gina came up to him. She was a fourteen-year-old sport-mad tomboy, who more than held her own with the boys at basketball, and

Peter thought she was eager for a game. But, for once, sport was not on Gina's mind. She said a neighbour had asked her if she knew any young boys with musical talent who wanted to become pop stars.

It was a conversation that sowed the seed of what was to grow into one of the biggest pop music phenomenons of all time, and today Peter remembers it well.

He said: "Gina told me that a woman, named Mary Alford, who lived in an apartment in the same house as her in St Gregory Street, wanted to start a group. Gina and I had grown up together, even dated each other in the sixth grade, and she knew I could act and sing a bit. So she said she was asking me first.

"I didn't immediately think, Hey, this is going to lead to something. But it seemed a pretty good idea at the time, and anyway, with the summer vacation ahead of me, I didn't have much else to do, except hang out in the park.

"So I said: 'Sure, I'll give it a shot.'

"Gina seemed really pleased. She said she was going to approach Donnie as well, and asked me if I knew anyone else with talent who might be interested.

"The only ones I thought would be interested were Chris Hagberg and Edward Russell, so I promised to talk to them. They were just as keen to give it a go and, a week later, all four of us went to Gina's house, just across from the park, to meet Mary Alford.

"I wasn't excited because I still didn't believe it was going to lead anywhere and I'm sure Chris and Eddie didn't either. But Donnie was quite geared up. We'd never had deep conversations about what we wanted to do with our lives, but I knew he fancied performing on stage. As we all walked to Mary's house, I'm sure he was thinking: 'This could be my big break.'

"Gina introduced us to Mary, who explained that she had a friend who was looking for five young good-looking boy singers with a lot of rhythm. She didn't say who he was – she just asked if she could hear us sing.

"I think we sang along to the current Prince hit – together at first, then individually. Mary seemed quite impressed and said

3

she would like us all to go to a house in Roxbury the next week to audition for her friend – all, that is, except Chris, who was sixteen and a couple of years too old for what Mary and her friend were looking for. They wanted young, cute-looking kids with sweet voices – and Chris's was breaking. Donnie told Mary his younger brother, Mark, would be keen to audition instead, and we all left and went back to the park, full of what had happened and what might be lying ahead."

What the boys did not know then was that the man they were to audition for in the dangerous district of Roxbury was Maurice Starr, a black record producer who had launched a successful black band called New Edition, which later set Bobby Brown on the road to solo superstardom.

Starr had lost control of the group in a legal battle with the MCA record company and was now anxious to promote a new Boston band. He had hit on an idea he was convinced could not fail: he wanted to find and groom five cute kids of no more than fifteen, who could sing contemporary black music. The only drawback was . . . they had to be white.

Mary Alford was an old friend, and when he bumped into her one day he told her his idea. Mary was excited. It was a winner, she said. The streets of Boston were brimming with young musical talent and she was sure that, out there somewhere, were five boys who fitted the bill. She left Starr that day, promising to help find them.

What neither Starr nor Mary suspected for a second was that, among the sports-crazy youngsters whiling away the hot summer days in Dorchester Park, was a fair-haired kid with the talent of five boys rolled into one; a boy who could sing and rap and break-dance and who, already, could hold an audience in the palm of his young hand. A boy years ahead of his time who was busting his gut to be a performer. A boy who, when he saw him, would take Maurice Starr's breath away.

A week after the audition Mary Alford pulled up at the park in her brown Mercedes to take Peter, Donnie, Eddie and

Donnie's brother, Mark, to Roxbury where Maurice Starr had a three-storey house near Dudley Station.

"I'll never forget that drive," says Peter. "I was only fourteen and had never been to Roxbury, but I knew all about its reputation as a violent area, with lots of muggings and stabbings and even murders. We drove through streets with garbage spilled all over the sidewalk and eventually pulled up outside what looked a derelict building. Suddenly, I was worried, perhaps a little scared. I thought: 'Whoa – what are we doing here?' Standing outside the building was a man in a large old navy blue coat, with a woollen hat pulled down over his ears. He looked like a bum, but as we got out of the Mercedes, he walked towards us and introduced himself as Maurice Starr. At that time, the name didn't mean anything to us.

"He told us he was in the process of turning one of his three floors into a recording studio, and took us to the top floor where I guessed he lived. He was very friendly and made us feel comfortable, very much at home. The four of us sat on a couch and he told us what he wanted to do. He was real cool and straight up. He laid it on the line. He said: 'I'm going to get a group together that's going to hit the charts. I want to find the talent that can do it. That's why you're here. I'm going to audition you. If you can do it, I'm going to keep you and we're going to go places.'

"He had a piano in the room and played a song, called Stop It, Girl. He then sang a few notes and told us to try to sing it exactly the same way. Eddie went first, then me and Mark, then Donnie, and all the time Maurice was listening intently, and studying our faces and movements.

"After we'd all had a go, he asked us if we had any other talents and Donnie told him he could break-dance. Maurice asked him to demonstrate and we went into another room where Donnie just got right on with it. He loved it and when Maurice asked if he could do anything else, Donnie said he could rap.

" 'Well, go on then, rap for me,' Maurice said.

" 'What do you want me to rap?' Donnie asked.

" 'Anything,' said Maurice. 'Do anything. Can you rap off the top of your head?'

5

" 'Sure,' said Donnie, confidently.

"And he just started rapping away, with no shyness or embarrassment whatever. It was like he was thinking: 'This is my big chance, and I must take it.' He rapped away non-stop for what must have been two minutes and all the time Maurice was standing there not knowing whether he could believe what he was hearing.

"When Donnie finally stopped, Maurice was grinning all over his face. Then he started clapping and said: 'Excellent, excellent. That's just what I'm looking for. We can use that. We can really use that.'

What Starr had been searching for were some white kids who had been raised among black people, who thought and felt the same way, and who could go into the ghetto and feel at home.

Donnie Wahlberg, he could see at once, fitted the bill perfectly.

Those who knew Donnie and his background would not have been surprised. For he was among the first children in the country to be taken to an all-black school under a Government integration plan. Donnie and dozens of other children were taken to and from the Trotter school by bus every day in what became known as the "bussing system." The aim was to encourage and improve racial harmony. All races and cultures were taught to mix in, work well together and treat each other with respect. And the school pioneered a new teaching programme which emphasised art and music. It all worked wonderfully.

From a very early age, most of Donnie's friends were black. He knew why they said and did certain things. He understood their moods and their humour. And, more important, he felt comfortable among them.

Musically, the black influence rubbed off on him at an early age. In Rose Holland, he had a black music teacher who made singing fun – a lively extrovert who found it impossible to stand still when she was conducting the school choir, of which Donnie was a member. She would not just clap – she would sway from side to side, feeling the beat through her whole body. She got her ninety-five children singing calypsos, spirituals and gospel hymns as well as traditional songs. And she would have them marching and walking and dancing to help them feel the beat, too.

In Rose Holland's happy choir, the children of all colours and creeds marched and sang and danced their hearts out for years, always enjoying it, and never realising it was becoming part of them.

So, when Donnie Wahlberg was asked to perform for the black man in the Roxbury ghetto, he didn't think about it, or falter, for a second. Because the black sound he had within him had been there for years. It was natural – even if he didn't know it.

Peter, Mark and Eddie were obviously not surprised at Donnie's performance. "He'd been entertaining us, and all our other friends in the park, for months," says Peter. "But he took Maurice Starr completely by surprise, not only because the rap was so spontaneously brilliant, but because it was a black voice coming out of a white body. Although we did not know it then, it was precisely what Maurice had been looking for. He was completely blown away by Donnie's performance and I'm sure he felt he could build a chart-topping band around him.

"When the audition was over, Maurice said we had potential and asked three of us to come back in a few weeks to start rehearsals. Unfortunately, he did not think Eddie was suitable because the band's image was to be cute and clean-cut and Eddie was a bit too big and manly.

"It was then that Maurice told us about his success with New Edition – a Boston band we'd all heard of – and for the first time I began to think: 'You know, this could go somewhere.' If I was more hopeful now, Donnie was really geared up about it. This was his *thing* and he was very, very happy about it. He couldn't stop talking about how great it was going to be. He believed in Maurice Starr from the moment he met him."

The boys left the roughness of Roxbury for the familiar air of Dorchester, Mary Alford's Mercedes noisy with their teenage excitement. Donnie and Mark and Peter were sad that Eddie was unwanted, but thrilled at the possibilities that lay ahead for them. They found it hard to contain themselves.

* * * * *

Sadly, Peter's mother did not share her son's optimism. When he proudly showed her Maurice's business card and told her about the audition, she was very sceptical – and horrified that he had been to a stranger's house in such a bad area. Peter told her about Maurice's connection with New Edition, but she was still wary and agreed to let him go back for practice and rehearsals on condition he didn't go alone. And she warned him that, no matter what, school work would have to come first.

Today, Peter's mother, Bernadette Fitzgerald, kicks herself that she was too negative and critical of Maurice Starr's motives.

"Yes, I was wary of the whole thing," she admits. "It just didn't sound right – all a little too easy. Peter did say Maurice Starr had been involved with New Edition, but my feeling at the time was that a man they had never met could have told them anything. They were gullible fourteen-year-olds and wanted to hear that this was their big chance to be superstars."

Mrs Fitzgerald agreed for Peter to carry on seeing Maurice, but first, a replacement had to be found for the "big and manly" Eddie. Mary Alford again sought Gina's help and Donnie told her he knew the ideal kid – a fast-talking rapper like himself, who could break-dance, too.

The boy's name was Jamie Kelley and Gina told Mary, who said:

"Fine, bring him along to meet Maurice."

Jamie and Donnie were friends before kindergarten, even though Jamie was two years younger. They did not go to the same school, but they carried on their friendship in Dorchester Park, playing ball games and hide and seek with other young-sters, and generally hanging out together. When the break-dancing craze gripped Boston, they teamed up into an exciting duo and won the respect of hundreds of other teenagers in the city's downtown clubs and dancehalls with thrilling, well-rehearsed routines.

Jamie, now nearly nineteen, says: "Donnie and I used to practise in each other's homes and in the park. Then, one Sunday, we went to the Club California in Quincy, to watch a lip-synching contest, and we couldn't help thinking we were better than all of the contestants.

"Throughout the next week we learned the Rock Box song, sung by Run/DMC, and practised like crazy every spare minute we had. We bought some dark glasses, put on our most fashionable clothes, and went back the following Sunday to take part in the competition. We won first prize – a fifty dollar savings bond each. It was simple."

Jamie, like Peter, was frightened when Mary's Mercedes drove him, Donnie, Mark and Peter into Roxbury. He had been told there was nothing to worry about, that Maurice was on the level and keen to make them stars. But Jamie was younger than the others and, despite his brash, streetwise personality, he was concerned at what he was letting himself in for.

Once up the dark stairway and into Maurice Starr's comfortable lounge, however, Jamie relaxed. When Maurice asked him what he could do, Jamie admitted he wasn't much of a singer, but was not slow to show off the break-dancing skills that had won him so much acclaim in the clubs. Maurice was impressed. He said Jamie was in.

"I was still not sure about it, but I found it hard to doubt Maurice Starr," Jamie admits today. "He said he'd already written songs for us and if we did everything he wanted, the rest would come in time. He warned us that it would be really hard work, but if we stuck with it, we would all be rich and famous. For someone just 13, like me, it was hard not to believe what I was being told, especially when Donnie, who I looked up to, was so positive about it all.

"Mary drove us back to the park and told us that Gina would let us know the date of our first practice.

"When I went back for my first practice I was still a little unsure. But, when I saw the studio, I started to believe in the set-up a bit more. There was a drum machine and all fancy instruments and, what had looked no more than an ordinary room, now looked like a proper recording studio. I was impressed. We listened to some tracks Maurice had already laid down and started working on a few routines.

"After that, we practised three times a week, after school, for between three and five hours each time. A choreographer named David arranged our routines and Maurice's brother sat at the piano and gave us singing lessons."

As that summer of 1984 wore on, sport in Dorchester Park for Donnie, Peter, Mark and Jamie took a back seat. And then it was time to return to school, and Peter Fitzgerald's mother made the decision that was to cost her son the chance of fame. Although she had not met Maurice Starr, she still felt his whole involvement "a little bit on the shady side." And, when Peter resumed school in September, she felt he could not afford to spend three evenings a week in a studio, when he had homework to do, particularly when the nights were drawing in and the studio was in a rough part of town.

"I always wanted Peter to concentrate on school and get good qualifications," she says. "I did not want him putting all his time and energy into what seemed like a fly-by-night operation, then be left with nothing when it didn't work out.

"To his credit, Peter understood my decision and didn't give me a hard time. That's his nature anyway – a really easy-going kid, who rolls with the punches. If performing with a band was something he really wanted to do, he may have put up an argument, but there was no scene. He just agreed and got on with his school work. He didn't keep tabs on the boys. He seemed to lose interest and, in fact, forgot all about the band until the New Kids became famous.

"It's hard to speculate on something that might have been. Of course, I kick myself that I was negative and untrusting and didn't give the thing more of a chance. But a mother has to do what she feels is right for her son. In the end, it was one of those things that *did* work out – but it could have gone the other way and left Peter high and dry with few academic qualifications to fall back on."

Today, Peter is philosophical about his mother's view. He

says: "I was fading out of the picture anyway when she made her decision. I would tell the boys I'd try to make practice, but school work kept getting in the way and I kept letting them down. It bothered me. If I wasn't putting in the time and effort, I felt I shouldn't ride on someone else's coat-tails. But my mom made the actual decision for me. She didn't want me missing school, not doing my homework and flunking subjects. I understood that. It was my first year in high school and she wanted me to do my best. She was the nurse there and if I didn't do well, she would hear it from my teachers.

"I didn't mind at all. It wasn't as if I was missing anything with the band. What they were hoping to achieve was potential – a pipedream – and I think she made the right decision, based on what she knew at the time. Mind you, that doesn't stop me giving her a hard time now when we see the New Kids on TV. I'll say, 'I'd be right up there with them if it wasn't for you!' We laugh it off. She knows I'm kidding her."

With Peter out and Maurice Starr keen to press on with practising, a replacement had to be found quickly, and Donnie told Mary he knew just the boy – an old pal from the Trotter school who had a lovely voice and could break-dance as well as anyone in Boston. He was also good-looking. The boy's name was Danny Wood.

2

Rivals in the Street

Danny, one of six children, had strict parents who instilled discipline in him to work hard at school. It paid off and, even at eight, Danny stood out above his Trotter classmates. He was so gifted that Barbara Jackson, who was headmistress for seventeen years, remembers him well: "He was a very bright boy who was particularly good at doing his homework," she says. "We had to put him on an advanced teaching programme, so that he was not slowed down by the other children."

Danny's talent was not restricted to academic subjects, however. He took a deep interest in music and when he graduated, Rose Holland presented him with a musical box – a little porcelain doll, wearing a cap and gown – as a reward for his hard work. The tune it played was We've Only Just Begun!

Rose was convinced Danny would use his musical ability when he was older. She says: "One year we had a party for all the girls and boys in the chorus and Danny and a black friend suddenly asked to go in front of the class and sing to a tape of a New Edition record. I was happy for them to do it. And I remember thinking they were so good it would be nice if they did something musically together when they grew up. But the black boy moved to a private school and nothing came of it."

To those who did not know Danny well, that impromptu performance may have seemed out of character. For he was a shy boy who was quiet and respectful and never spoke out of turn. When he was acting in school productions, however, he seemed a different person.

"On stage he came alive," says Barbara Barron, another of his teachers. "He had enough self-confidence to try out for all sorts of different roles, which he took very seriously. He had a stage presence – something that struck a nerve – even at ten."

This belief in Danny's star quality prompted Barbara to urge Danny's mother, Betty, to encourage him to go into show-business. After watching the boy play one of the Lost Boys in a school production of Peter Pan, Barbara told her: "Danny is so shy and handsome, he can't fail to be a heartbreaker."

For Danny, though, the stage took second place to the running track – and dreams of winning an Olympic gold medal. In addition to his academic and musical ability, he was a sports-crazy boy who belonged to an athletic club and competed over various distances.

Kelly Madden, who used to train with him as a kid, said: "We spent a lot of time together and got on well. I would gee him along if he was slowing down and tease him whenever I beat him in a race.

"We used to help each other out with exercises and encourage each other to keep going when they began to hurt. Danny was good fun, but he worked really hard at his fitness.

"We would chat about what we wanted to do when we grew up and he was always talking about training for the Olympics and winning a gold for America. Lots of young kids think that sort of thing, but both of us really believed we could do it."

Danny's self-discipline and dedication was evident even as a young teenager and when he was not at school or training for athletic competitions, he would spend many hours in the evenings, practising basketball at a net in his garden. But what the neighbours in Adams Street remember him most for is the patience he showed teaching local kids to break-dance for a summer show in his front garden.

Next door neighbour Lilian Dunleavy said: "He wanted to put on the best performance possible and he spent hours in the evenings and at weekends showing the kids how it was done. They were only seven or eight years old and couldn't pick it up as quickly or as well as Danny. But he showed great tolerance and understanding and when the day of the show arrived he had got them doing it perfectly. The whole street turned out to watch. We all thought it was great. Danny was such a lovely kid and had such a giving nature."

Danny was never one of the gang who hung out in Dorchester Park. But Donnie had been quite close to him at school and, at ten and eleven, they played indoor hockey and basketball, and swam together, at the Daniel Marr Boys and Girls Club, in the Savin Hill area. Later they renewed their friendship at the popular Dorchester Youth Collaborative – a meeting place for youngsters of all races – a few yards from the Hi-Fi Pizza restaurant at Fields Corner.

The decision to invite Danny to join the would-be band showed what vision Donnie had, even as a fourteen-year-old. For Danny's self-discipline and ability to dedicate himself to a particular project or pastime would prove vital in the coming months when the pressure to practise became even more intense.

But no sooner had Danny passed the Maurice Starr audition than the still unnamed band had yet another setback. Mark Wahlberg decided he preferred basketball to singing and broke the news to his brother that he was dropping out.

Donnie was shaken, but understood, and backed his brother's decision. Even so, a lesser person might have got despondent. Might have felt the odds of realising his showbusiness dream were stacked against him. Might even have quit and settled for entertaining the sporting crowd in Dorchester Park.

But for Donnie Wahlberg the yearning to be a performer, like his belief in Maurice Starr, was as strong as ever, and the thought of throwing away all he had worked for that summer did not occur to him. He had never been a quitter. And he was not going to start now.

He thought of all the boys he knew who had talent. And, if they had the talent, who would have what it took to knuckle down and practise, hard.

Donnie thought and thought. And then he picked up the phone at his home in Peverell Street, and rang Jordan Knight, a dark, good-looking boy he had got to know through Jordan's adopted brother – a black boy named Chris – who went to the same school.

Again, Donnie's intuition was stunning. Like him, Jordan was a great break-dancer. But, more important, he had the most exquisite falsetto voice.

One of Jordan's close friends, David Harris, was sitting in the Knight's mansion-like home on Melville Avenue, when Donnie's phone call came through.

"Donnie, by the sound of it, was very calm about the whole thing," David recalls. "He just said he was putting together a band and would Jordan like to be in it? Donnie certainly didn't say 'Hey, this is it, man, this is the big time.' But Jordan was very, very excited and accepted the offer on the spot."

Rose Holland would not have been surprised at Jordan's reaction. If she had seen the expectant grin on Jordan's face when he put the phone down, she would have smiled to herself. For Rose, more than anyone, knew that music was in Jordan's blood. It was the only profession she believes he would have been truly happy in.

"He seemed to be born with musical talent," Rose says. "His interest in school was high from the very beginning and, unlike most other boys, he was always willing to sing solo.

"He stands out most in my mind. I would go along rows of children, my ear down, listening to them sing, and I noticed early on what a beautiful voice Jordan had. Most of the singers in the school chorus were girls, but when I heard Jordan's voice he was one of my first choices."

Gorgeous though his voice was, Jordan saw more in music than just singing. He became interested in the piano and key-board, and when the school gave him the chance to take extra music lessons, Jordan jumped at it. "He couldn't wait to get to those lessons," Rose remembers. "He loved learning to play those instruments and he was always practising, sometimes three times a week."

That dedication continued when he and his brother, Jonathan, went to their middle school, English High. At the end of most days, there was a singing class, and, again, Jordan could not wait to get to it. The lesson would last for half an hour, then students could do what they liked for fifteen minutes. Jordan headed straight for a keyboard and was in a world of his own for the next quarter of an hour.

It was this single-minded dedication that made Jordan as good a break-dancer as Danny, who was one of a rival group of teenagers who break-danced outside stores in downtown Boston.

David Harris, says: "Jordan didn't like to ask his mother for money because he knew how tough she was finding things financially. So, every Saturday morning, the two of us and some of our friends would take a train into town, carrying a huge piece of cardboard – about 9ft by 8ft – between us. We would select a suitable store around Sumner Street, lay down the cardboard on the sidewalk, and start break-dancing on it, with cushions in our hats, so that we wouldn't hurt when we spun on our heads.

"We'd perform for half an hour or so, then move on to another store. By lunchtime, we'd have earned around forty dollars, which wasn't bad for thirteen and fourteen year olds. We'd split it up between us, then go off to eat. It was great fun and became a way of life on Saturdays.

"There were another two groups of nine kids working the stores and the rivalry was keen. Danny was a brilliant break-dancer, but Jordan wanted to be as good, and he practised until he improved to the point where there wasn't much to choose between them.

"The top break-dancer around in the mid-eighties was a Spanish guy from New York called Crazy Legs and Jordan would spend hours watching him on video and try to imitate him. There was a break-dancing movie around then, called Wild Style and all our gang – none more than Jordan – were wild about the soundtrack!"

The rivalry between the break-dancing groups was hard, but there was never any fighting on those Saturday mornings. Jordan was more likely to run into trouble on his own doorstep. For, although Melville Avenue, was an attractive, spacious road, with large houses costing more than $300,000, it lay between Washington and Dorchester Avenues – a tough multi-racial neighbourhood – and the threat of violence was constantly in the air.

"It really wasn't safe to walk the streets unless you kept your wits about you," says David. "Jordan was never the type to go looking for trouble, but sometimes it came looking for him. One Saturday morning, we got off the train at Shawmut station and were threatened by six black kids. It wasn't racial – they were hanging around with nothing else better to do and just felt like a bit of trouble. Jordan and I ran off, petrified, because the kids were all about three or four years older and we wouldn't have stood a chance in a fight. We dodged through all the back streets and managed to get home safely. But it was a close thing. Another time, we were chased from Town Field, on Dorchester Avenue, by another group of kids – white this time. It was a tough place to grow up in, that's for sure."

With less caring, socially-aware parents, Jordan and his brothers could have taken the wrong turning in those early years. With little to occupy them, kids would generally hang around street corners, looking for ways to relieve the boredom. Drug-taking was commonplace, even among thirteen-year-olds.

Although he was often out, Jordan was rarely seen idling his time away in the street. When he was nine or ten, you would find him in his back garden, riding his BMX bike over home-made jumps with Liam Hughes, whose home in Tremlett Street backs on to the Knight house. Later, Jordan threw himself into sport and was nearly always with other boys in Dorchester Park.

Teenagers, especially boys, are usually attracted to the arts or games – not both. One rarely finds a boy gifted musically, showing a flair for throwing or hitting a ball around, but Jordan had talent in both areas. He showed exciting promise in ice hockey and as a baseball pitcher and was good enough to play in leagues. He shone at basketball, too, and played regularly at Dorchester Park. But he never came into contact with Donnie and Peter Fitzgerald and their group.

Liam has fond memories of another, less obvious, side of Jordan's personality.

"He was a very caring kinda guy," he says. "When I was eleven or twelve, I was very small for my age and was always being picked on in the school yard. If I'd been in a fight, and was looking unhappy, Jordan would always be the first to ask me what was wrong and offer to help if I was hurt. I'll never forget him for that."

According to Liam, the younger Jordan was a bit of a clown, always ready for a joke. It is a view shared by Father Titus Oakes, a priest at All Saints Church, in the Ashmont district of Dorchester, where all the Knights sang in the choir.

"I remember Jordan well," says Father Oakes. "He was a cheeky little face in the choir, with a mischievous twinkle. He'd get a bit of trouble going, then disappear. I always had the feeling that if the choirboys were doing something wicked, Jordan was the start of it. I may have booted his rear end up the stairs a few times – affectionately, of course.

"You only have to speak to Jordan or his brother briefly to understand that they come from a family that places a lot of importance on good, moral Christian behaviour.

"They have been active parishioners all the eight years I've been in Dorchester. Helping people in need is a way of life for their mother, Marlene. She attends Bible Study groups, visits people less fortunate and has taken into her home many retarded children and adults. She is a shining example of Christianity in action.

"Jordan and Jon were distraught at the break-up of their parents' marriage, but they still took an interest in other people and were sensitive to their feelings. They could have been forgiven for feeling abandoned and sorry for themselves, particularly when their mother started fostering people in need to boost the family income. But, instead of complaining and feeling resentful, they followed their mother's lead and started taking an even deeper interest in the plight of others. A couple of years ago, Marlene took in an old man named Walter, who was in his eighties and unwanted by anyone. She cared for him like a loving relative for about six months before he died. Jordan and Jon were in tears at the funeral.

"No one knows the struggle Marlene had when she was left to bring up the children with no money coming in. But Jon and Jordan – and their brothers and sisters – responded magnificently and must take a lot of credit for helping their mother through a most difficult time.

"At the height of the crisis, Marlene said: 'We've got to keep this house together' - and her children rallied round. It was wonderful to see them all pulling together, particularly in a country where youngsters are keen to leave home as early as possible and get their own apartment. At one stage, Marlene was the only one bringing money into the house, but, even though they were only 12 and 14, Jordan and Jon worked downtown to help out."

One of those out-of-school jobs Jordan got was in a bank. And when he wasn't there or playing in Dorchester Park, he would more than likely be in the basement of his home, practising on his keyboard.

Donnie, quite simply, could not have thought of a better candidate to join them, nor chosen a better time to ask. If anyone was ripe to be picked for a shot at stardom it was Jordan Knight. And when Maurice Starr heard Jordan sing for the first time, he was knocked out.

Jamie Kelley, who was at the audition, says: "Maurice was real excited. He loved what he was hearing. He told Jordan, 'you're going to be a star.' "

As the summer of 1984 finally gave way to autumn, the would-be band still had a problem. The boys were learning how Maurice wanted them to handle his songs and they were enjoying working out the dance routines that would later thrill millions of the nation's young girl pop fans. But Maurice had set his mind on *five* good-looking, clean-cut boys – and he had only four. He wanted five and he was going to *have* five. Did any of the boys know anyone else? he wanted to know.

Again it was Donnie, self-appointed leader of the pack, who was first to come up with a suggestion – Jordan's brother, Jon.

3

The Gentle Gardener

Whether it was another flash of inspiration, or simply the first thought that came into his head, only Donnie knows. But it was to prove to be a wonderfully imaginative choice, because later, Jon would become a natural member of the band, with a magnetic stage presence. At the time, however, he seemed an unlikely choice. Jon's singing voice was not as good as his brother's, nor was he so involved in music. And while Jordan was the type to stop suddenly in the street and burst into an impromptu break-dance, Jon – a year older than his brother – was a less extrovert type who preferred the quiet life at home. He was more interested in plants than pop. The only dream Jon had was having enough money to buy a huge garden that he could colour with beautiful flowers. He poured as much energy into his garden as his brother did into music.

John Hughes, twenty-three-year-old brother of Liam, says:

"There was a lot of land in front and back of Jon's house and he loved to keep it looking beautiful. He would mow the lawn every two days, just to keep it neat.

"He was out there all the time, it seemed, planting trees and various bulbs. In the summer, I'd get up at ten o'clock and he'd be out there already. When I went in at five or six, he'd still be there, keeping himself busy. I've never known anyone get so much pleasure out of a garden.

"He was a real friendly and helpful guy. If I went into my own back yard, Jon would always come over and talk for a while before going back to his work. And he'd always be offering to help us move a branch or cut down a tree. After Hurricane Gloria made a mess of our garden a couple of years ago, Jon was right there, giving us a hand clearing up."

Jon's passion for gardening – and animals – helped him form a good friendship with a next-door neighbour. A couple of years ago, the woman's garden needed a good clearing up and she asked Jon if he would do the job, provided she paid him.

"I knew it would take quite a long time, so we agreed forty dollars," she said. "Jon started early and finished very late and I felt he had certainly earned his money. But he was out there again the next day and didn't stop for six hours. He was still going the next weekend . . . and the next.

"I couldn't believe his dedication. I said: 'Jonathan – you've used up that forty dollars, you know.'

"He said: 'Yeah, I know – but the job's not done.'

"He insisted on carrying on until he was satisfied. And he even built me something where I could dump all the rubbish. What a wonderful character."

Jon's back garden has a beautiful herbaceous border, which he designed after seeing Father Oakes working on one in his own garden at the church.

The priest, a dear friend of all the family, said: "Jon and I worked on our gardens together and have often swapped plants. He'd come to mine, look at a particular plant and say: 'Can I have a bit of that?' I'd say 'Okay – but can I have some of your delphiniums, lilies or whatever?'

"When the New Kids began to get successful, the boys all started talking about the spectacular houses they wanted to buy themselves and their loved ones. But all Jon thinks about is the garden and how he would adore one with a lake or a pond with fountains."

Not suprisingly, the naturist in Jon means that he loves animal life, and the Knights are legendary in the Melville Avenue area for the number of creatures which used to inhabit the family's front and back gardens.

Next door neighbour, Bill de Franc, who is the same age as

Jon, recalls that, at eight or nine, Jon had rabbits, chickens, goats, a husky dog – and a pony.

"At weekends, and sometimes on summer evenings, Jon's family would give local kids rides on the pony in the front yard," he says. "The Knight house was a pretty popular place."

Liam Hughes remembers that family even had a sheep. "How can I forget?" he says. "I was on the grass wrestling with Jordan when it joined in and started eating my hair! I wasn't crazy about sheep or any of the other animals, but Jon adored them."

Talk to school pals, teachers or neighbours or family friends and they will all say the same thing about Jonathan. What a caring, sensitive boy he was – and still is.

Father Oakes, who knows him better than most, says: "You never feel he is resenting you or getting impatient. He has enormous affection for people and always has time for everybody.

"People have always said that Jon is shyer than Jordan, but I'm not so sure. I've seen them at close quarters and I believe that, even though he is the centre of the band, Jordan is shyer. Backstage, he will go off to be on his own, but Jon will happily mix with everyone, no matter who they are or how old they are."

One of Jon's most endearing qualities that none of his fans would ever guess he has was discovered by one of his English High friends, Bertha White.

Bertha, who is two months older than Jon, met both brothers in Wainright Park, off Talbot Avenue, where she was part of a crowd that played basketball and generally hung around. She used to ride in the same bus to school, but never got talking to them until she was eighteen and in her senior year.

She returned to school in May 1986 after having a baby and, when she had some free time, she took the baby, Cassie, to see her sister, Colleen, who was working on a special course, called the Fenway Programme, on the tenth floor.

"All the kids usually went out there to use the phones and typewriters – including Jon," she said. "He kept coming in and I got to know him quite well.

"He got to know Cassie, too, and every time I went there he

22

would come into the office just to see her. He would take her from me and say: 'You're okay, you stay there and have a rest.' Then he would carry the baby around, showing her off to everyone. I didn't mind. Jon is a very gentle person and I knew Cassie was in good hands.

"He didn't do that with just Cassie. Other girls who had got pregnant would bring their babies to school and Jon would carry them off too. Having grown up with a lot of brothers and sisters, he's a real family type, who adores kids. I wouldn't be surprised if he's married and a father in a couple of years.

"People think he's shy, but that's because they don't know him. Once he's broken the ice with someone and feels confident with them, he'll open up and talk about anything you like. And while Jordan will never fail to say 'Hi,' Jon will always give you a hug everytime he sees you, as though he's really pleased to see you. He's very much like his mother in that respect. Not that I'm suggesting for a second that Jon is a mummy's boy. Far from it. He's just naturally affectionate and giving.

"At school, Jordan would rush out to be with his friends, but Jon would stay behind. You'd always find him in the secretary's office, answering phones, typing letters – even watering plants. If a teacher needed help with anything, Jon always seemed to be there. He was the helping type. It was his nature. He enjoyed it.

"The brothers were so different – Jon very down to earth, Jordan more of a playboy, always singing and laughing. I knew Jordan reasonably well, but if I had a problem, if I needed someone to talk to, I'd go to Jon every time. You could rely on him to listen carefully and give an honest opinion after considering all the options.

"They were different with girls, too. Jordan hardly ever associated with white girls; they were always Spanish or black. He always hung around with black boys, too. On the bus home, Jon would sit with me and our group of friends, but Jordan would be at the back with his black friends, making a lot of noise.

"When their band's first record came out, Jon was still at school. He and Jordan would pass cassettes around and we'd all kid them about their future. The record wasn't doing well, but it didn't seem to bother Jon as much as Jordan. He didn't seem obsessed with the thought of making it big like his brother. With all his interests, all those things that money can't buy that give him immense enjoyment and satisfaction, he knew it wouldn't be the end of the world if he didn't become a member of a top band."

This is why Jon did not get over-excited when Jordan mentioned that Donnie had asked if he wanted to join the band, that autumn of 1984. But he went along with it and, like Danny and Jordan, impressed Maurice at his audition. The starmaker now had the five boys he was looking for. All were under sixteen. All were good-looking. All had varying talents. And all were white. Now, all they needed was a name.

Many ideas were kicked around, but the one that stuck, the one that had a touch of mystique, an originality, was Nynuk.

4

Popeye and the Joker

It is not clear who thought of Nynuk. But the boys and Maurice were *all* guilty of making a terrible choice, for the name meant nothing and would serve only to embarrass the boys and confuse their fans. The boys did not know that at the time, of course. All that concerned – or, rather, excited – them was that all those hours of practise, both at Maurice's studio and in the basement of the Knights' home, seemed to be paying off. They were not merely a collection of individuals now – they were a band. And they had a name to prove it.

With Maurice promising to try to fix up a performance to see what they were like in front of an audience, the boys set their own publicity machine in motion – a graffiti campaign aimed at some some of the most prominent walls in Dorchester. Jamie, Jon and Danny were not that good at this form of free urban promotion, but Donnie and Jordan were brilliant.

"We wanted to spray the name Nynuk somewhere real big, where everyone would see it," says Jamie. "We looked around Dorchester for a couple of days and finally decided that the best place was on a train line used by thousands of commuters every day.

"Donnie, Jordan and I took a ride one day and scanned all the walls as the train flew by. We chose a spot near Savin Hill station and agreed to buy some colourful paints and meet up at nine o'clock that night.

"We took a train to Savin Hill, then climbed over a fence and waded through thick mud down the embankment on to the line. I was quite scared in an excited sort of way. But Donnie and Jordan didn't seem in the least bit bothered. They had the skill to lay down a design on paper, then reproduce it perfectly on a wall – and that night they set about the job like professional artists.

"They seemed to take forever. I kept looking around to see if we were being watched. I was quite jumpy. I was only thirteen, after all. Suddenly we heard the most almighty roar from a loudspeaker: 'GET OFF THE LINE.' It was the police. I ran off like hell. Donnie and Jordan followed, leaving the strange-sounding word, Nynuk, just about complete on the wall.

"We ran for about two miles. The police probably didn't even bother chasing, but we didn't think about that. The thought of getting caught – and our parents knowing – terrified us. We just kept running until we were puffed out and could run no more. After that, every time I was on a train and saw Nynuk on that wall I smiled to myself. But I wasn't laughing that night."

It is likely that Donnie, if not Jordan, *was* laughing. As a thirteen and fourteen-year-old, he was a practised graffiti artist and he chanced his arm in many areas of Dorchester.

Peter Fitzgerald, who was with him a lot of the time and admired his artistry, says: "Donnie took this form of art very seriously and would think nothing of spending half an hour on a drawing or sign. He did a couple of things up the park and a really fancy, colourful *JOKER*, with shadows, on the wall of a nearby high school.

"He got into calling himself Dexter P., for some reason. It was a sort of stage name and he used it in raps, like: 'Dexter P. – the place to be.' Around that time, you could see Dexter P. in graffiti in many parts of town. Jordan gave himself the graffiti nickname of Popeye. Don't ask me why.

"Donnie knew defacing public property was illegal and would worry about getting caught. But we were young kids and had our wits about us. When the police chased us, we always ran into the trees. We always knew where to hide. I guess you could say Donnie was daring and waited till the last second before running off – if you want to immortalise him!"

* * * * *

And still the hard work went on. Marlene Knight allowed her sons to stay up late and, even at midnight, the sound of Jordan's keyboard would fill the basement that his handyman brother, Jon, had helped turn into a mini recording studio. Donnie, Danny, and even the youngest, Jamie, had what the Americans call late "curfew" and the five of them would relentlessly practise the songs and style Maurice Starr had taught them. Because they now had a name, and the dream of performing was more of a reality, the practice became like a drug and the boys would send out for pizzas from the Hi-Fi, so that they could carry on working.

If Rose Holland could have been a fly on the wall at those gruelling five-hour sessions, she would have found Donnie's input staggering. For in those thirty-minute music classes at the Trotter school, only three or four years before, she had found it hard to get him to sing in front of the class.

"He wasn't dedicated at all," she says. "You could see his thoughts written all over his face – 'like when is this boring period going to be over?'

"It was difficult to know then if Donnie had any musical talent, because he was too busy talking. The room we used for music lessons was so small I had to cut out all conversation, or else we would not have had time for music. But it wasn't easy where Donnie was concerned. There'd be a general confusion, with one group singing one thing and another singing something else – with a noisy chat about what had gone on in the schoolyard in the middle! You could always bet Donnie was the one starting the confusion.

"Danny, Jon and Jordan were quiet, co-operative and deter-mined to please. But Donnie couldn't keep quiet and I was always having to tell him off for disrupting the class.

"I'd have to say sharply: 'Donald, time to stop talking – time to sing.' But it was quite obvious that he preferred talking to singing and, although he was never fresh or cheeky, it was clear he wanted to be at the centre of things. He was very strong-minded and always ready to speak up for himself."

As that 1984 winter drew on, however, the talking had stopped for Donnie Wahlberg. Well, slowed down, at least. He was still super confident, the self-appointed, if natural, leader of the pack; and he still was not slow to speak his mind – call the shots. But he was bright enough to know that no amount of talking was going to make Nynuk successful, like New Edition, Maurice Starr's former band, which was soaring higher and higher.

So, the talk made way for perfecting Maurice's songs and the dances that went with them. Donnie could see it all now, could see the stage beckoning, and nothing was going to stop him – or the band. They *were* going to be a success. He *was* going to be a star. Just like he'd always wanted to be.

Not many people thought Donnie would ever do much with his life. Why on earth should they have? Dorchester was a grim, low-income area with a high crime rate and the negative opportunities far outweighed the positive ones. The drop-out rate in schools was fifty per cent and the same percentage of girls became pregnant before they were eighteen. It was not unusual for well-behaved intelligent kids with high potential to get into the wrong crowd and go off the rails, even end up on the wrong side of the law.

It had happened to Donnie's elder brothers, Robert and Jim, and even Mark had appeared in court. Most folks were wary of the brothers, and gave them a wide berth. They were considered losers, unlikely to make a success out of anything and everyone thought they were all the same. Why, people wondered, would Donnie be any different?

Certainly Joe Gateley, who ran the Hi-Fi then, and served Donnie dozens of his favourite Italian pizzas, cooked on the brick, admits he did not care for the boy.

"He was different from all the other kids and I didn't like it," says Joe. "It was the way he handled himself. He was Mister Everything – very confident, cocky if you like.

"He was ahead of his time – the first kid to wear earrings, the first with a pony-tail. And he took such pride in his appearance he was always so much better dressed than the other guys. He'd wear jeans, sneakers and a dress-shirt like his friends, but he took such care of himself he always stood out. I wouldn't say he was flashy, but he was so well put together for a kid of his age, I didn't like it. People are threatened by change and I was no exception. Donnie was a trendsetter and so, so sure of himself. I'd think, Hey, who does this guy think he is?

"He was never rude. To be honest, I was probably rude to him, just for what he looked like, and the way he handled himself. He always wanted to be the centre of attention. I don't mean he flaunted himself or showed off. But he had just a little bit too much to say for himself. He tried to be too much of a nice guy for my liking, maybe because he felt he had to compensate for his family's name.

"Donnie was always in here, either with his friends and his family – or just by himself on Saturdays when he was on a lunchbreak from his uncle's store round the corner. Donnie was a worker. From a very early age, he was interested in making money for himself.

"I don't remember him telling me about Nynuk or his plans to be a star. But if he did I probably told him to forget it and do something to get his life together. I had such a bad impression of him, I didn't dream of him making it. I misread his confidence for arrogance and thought he was destined to follow in his brothers' footsteps."

That kind of negative talk would have cut no ice with Donnie. He'd always been a positive thinker and right now nothing was more positive in his mind. Bright enough to know the value of good grades, he continued to work hard at school. But he was flying high on his dream now, and nothing would convince him he was going to fall flat on his face.

Between school lessons and practising with the band, Donnie worked in the sports shop, owned by his uncle, Jack Malone, near the Hi-Fi. In quiet moments, Donnie would tell Jack about his dreams and how Nynuk was going to be big – bigger, perhaps, than even New Edition. But Jack, a hard-bitten grumpy man in his sixties, had no time for such wild day-dreaming and would laugh in his fourteen-year-old nephew's face.

Donnie took it all in his stride. Unwilling to argue, to try to convince Jack of Nynuk's potential, he just got on with his work, wishing away the hours until he could leave, around six, to rehearse with the band, either in Roxbury, at the Knight home or at the nearby Lee school. *He* knew the band were going to be big. And soon everybody else would know it. Too much hard work, too much hope, had gone into it for it to be otherwise.

Today, Jack Malone admits he was wrong.

He says: "Donnie kept telling me how big the band was going to be, but I thought he was just a crazy kid with his head in the clouds. I told him he should be spending his time thinking about getting a worthwhile job that would give him security. But Donnie wouldn't listen. He said he wanted to be a musician and was going to *be* one. I thought he was wasting his time and would never get off first base. But look who's laughing now. The kid I paid five dollars an hour is now a millionaire.

"I don't see Donnie any more. He's never in town with enough time to come and see me. I don't care. I'm sick of hearing about the band anyway."

5

Terror in the Park

Between Jack Malone's sports shop and the Hi-Fi, lies the Dorchester Youth Collaborative, known simply as the DYC by the 100 or so boys and girls who go there most afternoons and evenings. Donnie, Danny and Jordan used to meet there before going off to join Jamie and Jon for practice. DYC organiser, Emmett Folgert, an affable, easy-going guy in a baseball cap, remembers them as three well-mannered likeable guys who got on with everyone, no matter what race, colour or creed.

"They based their friendships on personality, not prejudice," he says. "They hung out with Spanish, black and white friends. They were very supportive and able to take support. Jordan started coming here when he was thirteen and in a break-dancing group, but Donnie and Danny didn't use the place until they were fifteen.

"The other kids here knew they were trying to develop a band, but neither Donnie nor the others were immediately accepted as stars of the future. Boston is full of young people with talent to entertain and, at the time, Nynuk was nothing but five young hopefuls who might, or might not, do something."

A code of behaviour drummed into young people at the DYC is to respect everyone and demand respect back, no matter where you might come from. Emmett won the respect of Donnie and Danny very early on and they were moved to tell him about their ambitions.

31

Unlike Jack Malone, and the other sceptics who did their best to dishearten them, Emmett was positive and encouraging.

"I told them to go for it," he says. "I knew they had been practising hard six days a week to fulfil their dreams, and felt that if anyone deserved success, it was them.

"They were all different personalities, which was a great strength. Jordan, I knew, was an artistic and dedicated singer, who would work for weeks on a certain style until he got it right.

"Donnie was a stone cold genius, a brilliant and versatile young man, who could get up in any hall and make a rap right out of his head. He did that at Salem State College in the break-dancing days before Nynuk. He just grabbed a mike and went into a rap, right off the top of his head.

"Danny was a stunning dancer who had the single-mindedness and self-discipline to do anything he wanted.

"I didn't know much about Jordan's brother, Jon, or Jamie Kelley, but I was sure Nynuk had the basic ingredients to be a smash. There wasn't anything like them around at that time.

"They said they wanted to be big stars with lots of money. But knowing them as I did, I had a strong feeling they were the types who would use that power for a positive purpose. I didn't feel fame and fortune would ruin them. They came from strong, level-headed families and had loyal, down-to-earth friends, who would keep their feet on the ground."

Once Maurice Starr was convinced the band had improved enough to be taken seriously, he arranged for all the boys' parents to go to his Roxbury home to hear the plans for them. They all sat in the lounge on the third floor, while the five boys waited in the studio downstairs.

Jamie's father, particularly, was pleased to be meeting Maurice.

"He hadn't been happy about all the time I'd been spending practising, and he was anxious to get a few things sorted out," says Jamie. "He had a big notebook, with lots of questions written down for Maurice. He asked them all and Maurice answered them. After the meeting, my dad was a lot happier. He trusted Maurice and was happy for me to keep going. That made me feel a lot happier, too, because, if I'm honest, I still had a few doubts, despite the positive attitude of the others in the band."

By now, the five schoolboys who were Nynuk knew Maurice Starr's song and dance routines so well they were aching to perform them in front of an audience. But that did not prevent them being nervous when the starmaker announced: "You're ready. I've fixed up your first show."

The talking and coaxing and practising and rehearsal was over. The moment they had been waiting for, working towards, had arrived. It was time to stop dreaming and wake up.

And suddenly, the young boys with talent and hope beyond their years were filled with self-doubt. *They* knew they were good. But would other people, a public they didn't know and who didn't know them, feel the same way? Would they be a success – or would they fail like so many expectant bands before them? Would all the hard work prove to be a waste of time, as Jack Malone and all the other sceptics warned them it would ? And would they have to abandon all hope of fame and fortune and just accept what future Dorchester offered them?

The setting for what Nynuk had to offer was the Lee High School, off Dorchester Avenue, where they had practised so many times in the last few weeks. Maurice Starr told his young hopefuls the news one day after practice at his studio.

"He just said we were ready to give it a crack," said Jamie Kelley. "He said he'd sorted out which dance routine we were to do, and was bringing in some backing singers to put his songs on tape. All we had to do was dance and mime. Donnie and I were not worried, because of the lip-synching we'd done to our break-dancing in clubs, but the others were not so confident. They didn't know what to expect.

"Maurice was aware Donnie was a natural leader and told him he was the one who would perform in front of the band – the one who would have to smile and get the crowd going.

"Donnie wasn't concerned in the least. He loved it. After all, he'd always been our leader, the one with the ideas, the one with the biggest dreams. It was as if Nynuk was his band, and he, not Maurice, was controlling it. From those days in the park, Donnie was always more grown up than the rest of us. He did the talking and had all the answers. And it seemed quite natural that he'd be the big draw, the one in the spotlight, with the four of us fitting around him. It was like being in the Army – Donnie was the captain and we were his lieutenants, waiting to carry out his orders."

The big night arrived and Nynuk, wearing glittering red sequined shirts and black trousers, took the Lee High School stage in front of nearly 400 people. It was just as well their costumes were sparkling, because their performance was not. They sang three numbers – Be My Girl, Stop It Girl and a rap called New Kids on the Block, which had been written by them – but the backing tape sounded tinny and it was obvious the band were miming.

The audience gave them lots of applause at the end of their final number, but Jamie Kelley is honest enough to admit the band did not deserve it.

"Thank God most of the audience were family and friends – because we were really terrible," he says. "Everyone was so kind because we were just starting out.

"The band were aware it was less than a satisfactory start, but we felt better when we saw that Maurice seemed pleased with the way it had gone. He kept telling us it was just the start, and not to worry."

What few fans know is that the band's first video was shot at that debut performance. One of Maurice's friends had a camera and filmed the boys from varying angles, then took different shots of the audience to make it look as though there were four thousand there, not four hundred.

"I must say that when he came in for the close ups of us dancing we really thought we were getting on the way," says Jamie.

On the way or not, it was back to the studio and the Knights' basement after that concert for more practising. The five of them were like brothers. They practised every night and stayed together at weekends. They were Nynuk and Nynuk was them. They lived and breathed the band and talked and thought about nothing else.

And then Maurice Starr told them he had fixed their next concert.

And Captain Wahlberg and his lieutenants almost froze in fright at the thought of it.

The venue Maurice Starr had chosen was Franklin Park, a huge, sprawling grassland with football fields, a golf course, even a zoo, on Blue Hill Avenue, in the heart of Roxbury. The occcasion was the Kite Festival, an annual event held every May, and attended by between 2,500 and 3,000 people.

Donnie and his pals were scared at the prospect because the Festival was chiefly a black affair and you'd be able to count the number of white faces in the crowd. What on earth were a horde of musically discerning black people going to think of five little white kids with loads of practice, but only one performance, under their young belts?

Over the next three weeks the boys worked even harder. And when they weren't practising, they talked about the Kite Festival. They tried to put up a front, but the more they thought about it, the more nervous they got. It was, they felt, like sending lambs to the slaughter.

In the event it was worse, far worse, than any of them could have imagined. And, had it not been for Donnie's courage, The New Kids on the Block may never have happened and Nynuk may never have sung and danced another number.

Jamie Kelley, just thirteen at the time, says it was a terrifying day he will never forget.

"Maurice hired a white limousine from one of his friends to take us to the park," he says. "It made us feel special and helped to take away some of our tension. But when we arrived at the park and saw the enormous crowd, we started getting nervous all over again. We just couldn't believe it. The park was huge and there seemed to be people as far as our eyes could see.

"When we saw what we were going to have to dance on, we didn't know whether to laugh or cry. It was not a proper stage, just a few dozen tables pushed together on uneven worn grass. There wasn't even a board over the top to provide a flat surface.

"The thought of performing on that didn't do much for our nerves, but then we were told we were going on last, and we began to get real jumpy. It meant we would have longer to think about the ordeal.

"We waited and waited and then, late in the afternoon, it was our turn to go on. We jumped up on the tables in the same red and black costumes we'd worn before and started dancing and miming to Stop It, Girl. It didn't go down too well, but we shrugged it off and went straight into our second number. We didn't get very far into it. The crowd hated us. They started chanting 'Off . . . Off. Get off the the stage.' Then they started throwing things at us – first, large clumps of earth, then stones. We didn't know what to do. We tried to carry on, battle through it, but, in the end, we ran for cover. We were petrified.

"Looking back, the whole thing was bizarre. Our backing tape was still running, but there was no one on stage to dance to it. We had a conflab at the side of the stage. Everyone seemed to be talking at once. Maurice said we had to be prepared to struggle to get to the top and was urging us to go back on. But we were so frightened we were, quite literally, shaking. We didn't know what the crowd were going to do. We were scared they might come on the stage and attack us. No one really knew what to do."

Finally, Jamie says, Donnie took over. Calm as you like, he walked back on to the stage and took the microphone. Someone had switched off the music, but the crowd was still noisy. It was as though they were baying for blood.

Donnie put his hands up, appealing for quiet. He didn't get it. "Excuse me," he said. Then, louder: "Excuse me. *PLEASE*."

Curiosity filled the air. The noise died to a rumble of discontent; the hostile crowd wanted to hear what this cheeky white kid had to say. Donnie gulped and took a deep breath. When he spoke, above the disgruntled murmurings, his voice was loud and clear, with the merest hint of arrogant defiance.

"We *are* going to finish this concert. If you don't want to listen, there are many other things here you can do. But we came to do what we do – and we *are* going to do it."

Jamie says: "The crowd didn't know what to make of that. They were surprised, that's for sure. And a bit impressed with Donnie's guts, I guess. Anyway, they all shut up and back on we went, to some ironic cheering. This time, they gave us a chance and Danny grabbed it. He started his voice beat box – drum and bass noises through his mouth – knowing the crowd would like it. They did.

"To finish, we lip-synched to the rap, The New Kids on the Block. The crowd went wild. They loved it. They just couldn't believe a white band – and one so young – could rap so well, and when we finished, they cheered and cheered. If it had been an indoor concert with seats, I'm sure we would have got a standing ovation.

"Donnie was incredible that day – so brave to go back on and face the crowd like he did. They respected him for it. That's why they shut up and gave us another chance.

"But one thing's for sure. Not one other member of the band would have done what Donnie did. And if he hadn't had so much guts, who knows, maybe our musical careers would have been finished before they'd properly started."

As it turned out, something happened later that day that would mark the beginning of the end for Jamie himself. Something that prompted Maurice's friend, Mary Alford, to think that, if Nynuk was to go on to the big time, Jamie was not suited to go on with them.

"There's no doubt about it – I upset her when we were in the limo, about to leave Franklin Park," he says. "There was an important basketball match I wanted to watch on television, so I asked the driver to switch on the set in the back of the car.

Mary, who was sitting next to him, told him not to. I couldn't believe it. I asked again. But Mary said: 'No.'

"I said: 'That's really cheap.' And she got really mad and gave me a lecture about being cheeky to Maurice's friends. She said Maurice had been kind to us, paying for the car and everything, and I was out of order.

"I didn't let it bother me too much, but Mary didn't like it. She'd never had much time for me anyway and this just made things worse. She never forgot that incident."

The end for Jamie Kelley would come a few months later. For the moment, the band were high on what they had done. They had ventured into black man's country, and won the day. They had turned a disaster into triumph. They had been a success. And the sensation, like the one they felt driving in the white limo, was sweet.

They took a sign for Dorchester. But for the young kids of Nynuk the only direction they wanted to go was . . . *UP*.

6

Farewell to a Dream

The feeling of jubilation gave the band the incentive to throw themselves harder into perfecting their act. And several weeks later, when Maurice told them their next concert was at "The Nine" in Dorchester's Lansdowne Street, the boys were delighted. The nerves that had jangled at the prospect of playing the Kite Festival were calm. After the horror of that performance, "The Nine", they all agreed, would be a piece of cake. Excitedly, they started to count the days.

Word had spread that Nynuk had something special and hundreds turned up to see if it were true. Donnie and Co. did not let them down and went through nearly every number they had learned from Maurice Starr. Although they were still lip-synching and dancing to a backing tape, the teenagers packing the club loved them and the boys left the stage to rousing cheers. Any lingering doubts that the band did not have what the young people of Dorchester wanted were dispelled that night.

And yet, such promise of a golden showbusiness future did not hold much for Jamie Kelley.

He was now fourteen, only one year older than when he had met Maurice Starr. But it was an age that made him aware of many distractions, such as girls and parties and alcohol. If Jamie had been a different character, if he'd had the vision to look beyond what was happening at the time to what might happen in the future, he might have resisted the temptations of youth and dedicated himself to the band like Donnie, Danny and the

39

Knight brothers. As it was, he convinced himself that he'd been missing out on the good things of adolescence and decided to put that right.

"Everyone in the band had become inseparable, going everywhere, and doing everything, together and I became bored with them," he says today. "All they would talk about was the band this and the band that. I got fed up.

"I was a teenager, but I hadn't done what most teenagers do. I'd been trapped like a virtual prisoner, practising all the time, and I needed to get out and do something different – have some fun, if you like.

"I started hanging out with a different crowd, going to parties, getting drunk, mixing with girls – you know, doing all those things a kid does when he's growing up. The boys in the band weren't into that. Maurice Starr had drummed into them the importance of a good, clean image and dedication, so, when they weren't practising, they were happy to go to the movies or stay at home and watch a video.

"The more I indulged in what I thought was the good life, the more I enjoyed it. And the more I enjoyed it, the less important the band became. Being picked up by Mary to go to practise had once been a joy – something I looked forward to. But now it had become a chore which I dreaded.

"I began driving a wedge between me and the other guys by ducking out of these practices. Instead of waiting for Mary to pick me up after school, I'd go to the park, leaving my mother to make an excuse for me. Other times, I would phone up and tell Mary, or one of the band, that I had to do something important and couldn't make it. I told all sorts of lies to get me out of rehearsals.

"I would turn up at, say, one out of three sessions. Understandably, the guys started getting uptight with me, because they couldn't rehearse properly with one member of the band missing. To make matters worse, singing lessons were improving their voices, but mine was still the same – pretty rough. I was acutely embarrassed."

Embarrassment, however, did not change Jamie's attitude. He continued to skive and lie and generally upset everyone connected with the band, until, finally, someone had to say something. Strangely, for once, it was not the talkative Donnie, but Jordan.

"I'd been slowing them down," Jamie recalls. "If I'd missed a session, where they'd been taught something new, it would take me some time to pick it up. One evening, we had to repeat a long routine *EIGHT* times before I got it right. All the guys were shouting at me, 'Jamie, what the hell are you up to?'

"Afterwards, Jordan pulled me to one side and said angrily: 'I'll give you one more month with the band if you carry on like this, Jamie.'

"If it was meant as a friendly tip, it didn't sink in. I still turned up for practice when it suited me and made some excuse when it didn't. I was selfish and arrogant, sure, but, hell, I was only fourteen and I wanted to enjoy myself.

"Almost to the day after Jordan's prediction, Mary Alford came to my house. It was one of those days it suited me to practise, and I ran out of the house and got in her car.

"But Mary shook her head. 'It's no good, Jamie,' she said, stiffly. 'You're out. You're not coming, even if you want to.'

"I was shocked. I knew I'd been unreliable and a pain in the butt, but I honestly didn't think they'd get rid of me. It wasn't as if I'd had any strong warnings to buck up – or else. Jordan was the only one who'd said anything and I certainly didn't take his comment as an official warning.

"To be honest, I wasn't bothered one bit. I didn't want what the other guys wanted badly enough. Deep down, I'd wanted out but hadn't known how to go about it. So I'd just done what suited me until they'd got so fed up they had to do something.

"I looked at Mary and grinned. 'Okay,' I said, 'no problem. See ya.' Then I got out of the car and ran over to the park, happy to have my freedom. At the time, I felt a weight had been taken off me, because I'd never enjoyed telling lies. But, maybe, I should have behaved differently. I took the bad road, while Donnie and the others took the good one."

* * * * *

41

Whether Jordan knew that Jamie was on borrowed time and was giving him a friendly warning is not clear. Certainly such a no-nonsense businessman like Maurice Starr is unlikely to have let things drift. With so much time and effort, if not money, invested in Nynuk, he could not afford any passengers – he would have wanted things sorted out one way or another. If Starr did decide to give Jamie a month to prove himself, he probably told the rest of the band, prompting Jordan to tip off Jamie to buck up his ideas.

What *is* certain is that with Franklin Park and the Lansdowne Club having given the youngsters valuable experience, Starr wanted to keep the momentum going. He had his sights set on more Boston club dates, then a record deal. That's what he had done with New Edition. Now, in the summer of 1985, he needed a replacement for Jamie – and quickly.

7

The Angelic Tearaway

If Maurice had wanted just a good-looking fifteen-year-old who could sing in tune and move sweetly, he could probably have found one the same day: Boston was brimming with young talent waiting to be discovered. But he wanted someone special – a *very* young boy who would give the band an added appeal, rather like little Jimmy Osmond and Michael Jackson had done for their big brothers in the seventies. The boy Maurice had in mind would be twelve, look cute and have the voice of an angel.

One day in June, Mary Alford told him that she'd heard of not one, but two, angelic kids who fitted the bill.

Which is how she came to be sitting in Jamaica Plain, a wealthier part of Boston, in a church hall one Friday night, watching Jonathan Shine and his pal, Joey McIntyre, rehearse for a musical for an amateur theatre group. One of Mary's friends had seen them sing in a show at the town's Footlight Theatre a few weeks earlier. She had been impressed.

When Mary saw them for herself she was impressed, too. And pleased. Both boys were just what Maurice Starr was looking for.

After the rehearsal, Jonathan and Joey were introduced to Mary, who told them about Maurice Starr and his plans.

The boys had been bemused by the stranger in the stalls, watching them rehearse. Now, they were excited. Could they come over to Roxbury for an audition the next day? Mary wanted to know. "You bet," said the star-struck pals in unison.

43

The next day, Joey's parents drove the boys to Starr's studio.

Today, Jonathan says: "We'd never been to Roxbury and were a bit nervous because of all the stories we'd heard about murders and muggings. But the audition itself didn't bother us at all – we had performed on stage so much. We didn't know what to expect, but we were kinda excited about the whole thing because of what Mary Alford had outlined.

"Inside the studio, we were introduced to Maurice Starr, who also gave us a run-down on what he was looking for and what he hoped to do. He sat down at the piano and sang a couple of lines from a song he'd written, Be My Girl. Then he told us he wanted us to sing the same lines for him.

"I went first and let my voice go. I was quite happy with what I did and Maurice seemed so, too. Then it was Joey's turn. His voice was much higher than mine and Maurice, Mary and some other people there liked that a lot. They asked if my mom or dad could drive over and fetch me, because they wanted Joey to stay.

"I was disappointed. But I wasn't angry with Joey or anything. They just preferred his singing to mine – and I suppose they were right. Joey and I are such good friends, I was pleased for him. Later that evening, when he'd returned from Roxbury, he came to my house. 'Hey, too bad about that,' he said. 'I'm sorry.' That was nice of him."

Jonathan would not have been surprised at that attitude.

Joey always won people over with his charm, even if he had scored a victory at their expense.

But he was strong-minded with lots of faith in his own ability – a strength of character Joey would need to draw on in the coming months. For although Maurice thought he was a wonderful asset to Nynuk, the rest of the band resented Joey for replacing Jamie and gave him a hard time.

Donnie, particularly, teased Joey and tried to embarass him by nicknaming him 'Bird' because of his bird-like features. Being the youngest by several years, Joey found it hard, but he battled to prove himself, and to show that not only did he have the talent to help them, but he had the dedication, too.

* * * * *

Anyone who knew little Joey McIntyre well would not have bet against him winning the band over. For even at age of five, the fair-haired, cute-faced kid showed a natural flair for entertaining people and had a sparkling personality to complement his talent.

Some weekends, the parents of Joey's best friend, Paul Callaghan, would invite several families to a meal at their house in Dunster Road, Jamaica Plain, not far from the McIntyre home in Orchard Street. Mrs Callaghan would normally kick off the after-dinner entertainment with an impromptu Charleston in the kitchen – and little Joey would stare at her, transfixed.

"Again . . . again," he would beg. "Do it again." And Mrs Callaghan would oblige, much to her guests' amusement and Joey's pleasure. The next step, of course, was to teach him how to do the strange "kicking" dance that had been so popular in the twenties. Joey picked it up in no time.

Today, Paul Callaghan's twenty-year-old sister, Paula, remembers: "Joey and my brother were little extroverts – they adored performing and showing off. My mom and I taught both of them the Charleston and they were fabulous – especially Joey. He would stand up on a chair in the kitchen and dance away. At first, he couldn't master the steps, but he watched and listened and, in no time at all, was doing the routine perfectly. He was so funny and cute – we laughed our heads off."

Joey, it seems, inherited his talent from his mother, Kay, a keen amateur actress who was involved in a local theatrical group herself. Her influence and encouragement helped, of course, but it was Joey's big sister, Carol, who introduced him to the talented stage teacher who would bring out the star quality that so impressed Mary Alford.

Carol was a keen member of Boston's Neighbourhood Children's Theatre, and every Friday night she rehearsed plays and musicals in a hall beside St Thomas's Church, near Orchard Street. One day, when Jocy was eight, Carol took him with her to sing for Michelle McCourt, an actress with a performing arts degree who was running the group. Carol believed her brother had exceptional talent. She wanted to know what Michelle thought.

What happened in the church hall that night was to shape little Joey's destiny.

"He came in, holding his sister's hand," Michelle remembers. "He was adorable – the sort of child you want to sit on your lap and tell you a story. He had short blonde hair and big blue eyes – very cute. He was quiet and well-mannered and, that day, shy and nervous, too.

"I auditioned Joey just as I do all other kids and asked him to sing a song every kid knows – Happy Birthday. When I heard him, I was astounded – completely knocked out. It is very, very rare for a boy of his age to sing that song in tune, but Joey sang it absolutely perfectly. He had a penetrating voice that really stood out above the others. I was really impressed and told him so. He was very happy.

"When I lined the children up in a choir I put Joey in the front row. I got them to sing several songs, and I could hear the quality of his voice above all the others. He was really throwing himself into it, not just going through the motions like so many kids do. He really did stand out as someone with a lot of promise."

It was that promise which, just one year later, would earn Joey an audition on Broadway.

Michelle had been impressed with him in his debut performance – a minor role in The Roar of the Greasepaint, The Smell of the Crowd – and decided to cast him in the title role of the musical Oliver!, with Carol playing the female lead. Although he was only nine, Michelle felt he was up to it. Joey did not let her down: he picked up his lines and the choreography brilliantly and rehearsed as hard as anyone.

She was thrilled by his performance in front of 350 people at Jamaica Plain High School.

"I always knew he had natural flair, but suddenly I became aware of his exceptional stage presence," she says. "I was so impressed, I rang a friend who is involved in theatre in New York. I felt Joey was good enough for an audition on Broadway.

As luck would have it, there was an ideal show for him. Ironically it was called Nine, and the producers had not cast the leading role.

"I felt it would be terrific for Joey just to experience a Broadway audition, so I drove him to New York. He wasn't nervous in the least – a little apprehensive that he'd forget the words of the song he had to sing, but that was his only worry. To be honest, he didn't seem to think too much of what was going on.

"Unfortunately, I wasn't allowed to see the audition, so I don't know how Joey presented himself. Certainly the director said he liked him a lot. But Joey didn't get the part, unfortunately. The director was looking for a dark-haired, Italian-looking boy and, of course, Joey is fair."

Far from being put off by the disappointment, Joey accepted it as part of his growing up and threw himself more and more into acting, playing the lead in such shows as New York, New York, Oklahoma, Hansel and Gretel, the Music Man and The Wizard of Oz. He also played one of the Von Trapp children in The Sound of Music. And when the theatre group put on shows at Disney World, in Florida, Nashville, Tennessee, California and Washington, Joey's determination in learning lines won him the admiration of his acting colleagues. Chosen to play a goose in Babes in Toyland, Joey excelled his own high standards. Michelle's husband, Allyn, who is an off-Broadway actor, coached him for the part and was astonished at the dedication of one so young.

"The goose part was so odd, compared with what he'd done before, and Joey worked particularly hard to get it right," says Michelle. "He would spend hours listening to and watching my husband. He wanted to walk, talk and dance like a goose and took everything in. He learned a great deal about acting in that role.

"I always felt Joey would make good use of his talents. He was an all-rounder – singer, dancer and actor – and so hard-working. Although he was a local celebrity in Jamaica Plain, long before New Kids, he was never self-centred, and I'm sure he'll never change. He is a wise young man, not the sort to let fame go to his head."

To Michelle, cute Joey McIntyre was always an angel. She had even picked him to be an altar boy at her wedding. But to people around Orchard Street, Joey was a mischievous little rascal, a tearaway whose devilish games with Jonathan Shine and Paul Callaghan caused all kinds of trouble in the neighbourhood.

Joey, who went to St Mary's Catholic School, in the Brookline area of Jamaica Plain, would team up with his pals when they were let out of their school. They gave themselves nicknames, which they still use today. Joey was Cloey, Paul was Cally and Jonathan, for some reason, was Deny. They even had a name for their favourite food – a heavily-packed sandwich of tinned spaghetti, which they would cook themselves. They called it "abiscus".

They played basketball and baseball and, although they were just twelve, they loved fooling around on mopeds in Arboretum Park. Bikes are not allowed in the park, but the boys used to sneak in and amuse themselves until they were spotted and told to get out.

They also invented naughty games, none more so than a favourite – called "Mookalaka" – which involved them standing on opposite sides of the street and throwing sticky plant buds at passing cars.

The object of the game was to see who could get the most buds to stay on cars. Once they had scored a hit, they would duck for cover behind a convenient bush or tree, so that the driver would not know what had happened. If drivers spotted them, they would run off.

Joey was a good shot and often hit cars. But, once, he was too slow to hide. The driver saw him and stopped. He got out and chased Joey.

Paul Callaghan, who was on the other side of the street, says: "The man pushed Joey to the ground and started grabbing his clothes and shouting at him. He was really screaming mad. I was worried sick, because I didn't know what the man was going to do. But after a couple of minutes he got back in his car and drove off. Joey and I found it exciting when we thought about it later, we laughed about it. But at the time we were scared."

Another time, Paul's father, Paul Snr, who owns a clothing shop nearby, had to ban Joey and Jonathan from his house after catching them playing with matches in the basement.

He said: "They had been in the house making a racket, then it went all quiet. I wondered what they were up to and started looking for them. Finally, I went down into the cellar and, sure enough, there they were, lighting candles.

"I went wild – they could have destroyed the place. I ordered Joey out of the house and told him not to come back for at least two weeks. I was very angry and he was shocked. He ran off all upset, saying he was sorry.

"They were always up to mischief and causing trouble. I would go crazy with the number of windows they'd break, playing baseball in the street. Neighbours would come screaming to me to get Joey and Paul inside, out of trouble. When the windows were smashed, I'd have to send both boys round to fix them until a glazier could be found. I lost count of the number of windows they shattered.

"Cars weren't safe either. Joey and his pals played football in the street, too, and were always banging and denting parked vehicles.

"He was a rascal, like any normal kid growing up, but he also had a lovely nature – considerate and kind. One day, Joey did something naughty to upset my wife. She shouted at him and told him to get out of the house. The next day was Mother's Day and my family went out for a while. When we came back, there was a rose on the back porch, with a note from Joey to my wife, saying he was sorry. He could be charming like that."

If trouble seemed to follow Joey around as a young kid, so did the girls.

As a sort of local personality, playing the lead roles in the theatre group's productions, he had no shortage of admirers. In fact, at the age of ten, says Michelle McCourt, he had a "harem" of up to twelve girls who were always fussing round him – even at rehearsals. On more than one occasion he would create such a stir of excitement, it brought the class to a standstill.

Says Michelle: "Joey was so sweet, the girls could not resist him. When he was around, you knew a certain collection would be there, too, huddling round him, chatting and smiling at him. Often, I'd be trying to organise a song routine, or a scene from a musical, only to find some of the class paying no attention at all, because they were more interested in Joey.

"He has seven sisters, so he was always used to girls' company and liked all the attention. But, one day, it got out of hand. It was disturbing the whole rehearsal, so I sent him home. I told him I didn't want him there any more. He was very upset, but I had no choice. A couple of days later he came round to see me and asked if it meant he shouldn't come to rehearsals *EVER* again. He was very worried and upset that he had been naughty. I put his mind at rest that I wanted him out of just that lesson, not forever. He was much happier after that."

One of Joey's favourite haunts was outside the Lil Peach, a small grocery and magazine shop in Centre Street. He and his pals would hang out there every day, sometimes for hours on end, and talk about all the things they were going to do when they were older; all the wonderful places they were going to visit. At that time Joey was crazy about football – American-style – and would tell his friends that he wanted to be a professional quarter-back.

As a kid, Joey loved football passionately and took it so seriously that he'd argue every disputable point until it was awarded his way.

"No one ever won an argument with Cloey during a game," says Jonathan Shine. "He would never give up any fight until he got his own way. Cloey was quite stubborn like that.

"He was very athletic and good at most sports. We were all into music in terms of the shows we did, and we liked listening to records and watching movies on TV. But, really, we were all the kind of kids who couldn't sit still and wanted to be doing something active."

But now, Maurice Starr was in Joey's life, and he had painted a colourful picture of a magical world, of fame and fortune, that far exceeded the wildest dreams Joey had swapped with his pals outside the Lil Peach . . . a world that could be within his grasp if he showed the same determination and dedication that had made him such a leading light in the amateur theatrical world.

So, as that summer of 1985 wore on, Joey had to put his future before his friends. Sport in the street started taking second place to band practice.

Paul's dad summed it up: "The boys would be playing baseball in the street when Joey's mother would drive up and say: 'Come on, practice time.' Reluctantly, Joey would leave in the middle of the game. You could tell he wanted to stay, but, deep down, he knew he had to go."

The sweet-faced kid with stars in his big blue eyes was sad to see less of the boys he had had so much fun with. But it was his destiny to follow the dream that the Roxbury starmaker was so sure would become reality.

8

New Kids go to Jail!

Now, the sound of music and youthful ambition rose even stronger from the basement of the Knight's rambling home and echoed around Melville Avenue for four to five hours every night. Yes, there *was* resentment towards Joey. And, yes, the tension did make practice difficult at times. But the band were bright enough to realise that the little twelve-year-old was good for them. Okay, he did come from a richer part of town. Yes, he did have a father who was a big noise in a powerful union. And, yes, he had replaced their friend, Jamie Kelley.

But they knew Maurice Starr was right when he said Joey's golden voice and angelic looks were just what the band needed.

And, unlike Jamie, he *was* reliable. He never missed practice. He listened to what he was told. And he seemed to want to make it as much as them.

Now, Mary Alford would drive to Jamaica Plain and take Joey to Dorchester. She would go down into the Knight's basement with him and the other guys and listen as they strove to perfect their art. She explained things they didn't understand. She positioned the microphones to fit in with their routines. She went out for sodas and milk and organised the pizzas.

And she was always there to boost them up when fatigue brought them down.

By the autumn, not long after Donnie's sixteenth birthday, Maurice Starr told the band the news they had been longing to hear: they had improved enough to lay down a tape which he would send to some record companies. He was confident of clinching a deal. After all, wasn't it he who had discovered Bobby Brown and New Edition? Donnie and the band were elated. This is what they had been working for. They kept studying hard at school, but in their hearts they knew they wanted musical acclaim more than academic success. They kept up their practising, all the time praying that the record companies would like their sound.

While they were waiting for a reaction, a subject that had been bothering Maurice and the band for months was finally brought into the open. It was the band's name.

No one liked Nynuk. It was a bad name. In fact, it stank. They all agreed it should be changed. But to what? It is not clear who, but someone said the rap they had been singing as Nynuk summed them up. The rap was The New Kids on the Block. And that, they all agreed, was what they were. They were new kids to the industry, soon to be new arrivals in the pop charts. More important, hadn't that been the number that had saved the day in Franklin Park? The number that had turned the jeers to cheers and made that hostile crowd aware that they were, indeed, a band to be reckoned with.

The New Kids on the Block. It was good. It was apt. And it appealed to everyone – Maurice, Mary, Donnie, Danny, Jordan, Jon and Joey – and others who were now playing minor parts in shaping the band's future.

Nynuk was buried without tears. The New Kids on the Block was born amid whoops of excitement at the dazzling future that lay ahead.

And then Maurice Starr told them they were to perform live in Boston's oldest, ugliest jail.

And for The New Kids on the Block, the fear they had felt at the Kite Festival jangled their nerves again.

The jail on Deer Island, in Boston harbour, is like something out of Dickensian London. Outside, the dark forbidding walls are weather-beaten and cracked. Inside, the antiquated plumbing is awful and the smell from the cells worse. The jail is a disgrace and a local judge is trying to close it.

But to the New Kids on the Block it was wonderful.

The apprehension that knotted their stomachs before their performance vanished when they ran on to the stage and into a warm, friendly atmosphere. All their numbers were greeted with rousing cheers from hundreds of appreciative prisoners and the band left the stage to cries of "More : .. More." On the way back to the mainland, the five young kids looked at each other with huge, satisfied grins. Performing in jail. What an experience! Had *they* really done *that*!

The New Kids started playing Boston clubs. Encouraged by the band's success in Franklin Park and Deer Island, Maurice Starr deliberately picked venues in predominantly black areas. If they could please the black man in his own back yard, he reasoned, they could perform anywhere.

The boys were welcomed in some clubs, but in others a black sound coming out of white mouths – even Donnie's brilliant rapping – was not so much a novelty as a joke. Behind their backs, some cruel cynics sneered at the New Kids, calling them "wiggers" – white niggers. The band got to hear this, of course, but were not the types to be put off. As Donnie had told the crowd in Franklin Park: "This is what we do and we're going to do it." So, while white bands stuck to heavy metal music, the New Kids continued to sing it their way.

It was not an easy time. They had put in so many hours, weeks, months of practice but even the merest hint of a break-through was not there. They broke up from school for the 1985 Christmas vacation and went back to the Dorchester Youth Collaborative and sought encouragement from their friends and bought pizzas from Joe Gateley in the Hi-Fi, and, as they celebrated Christmas with their families, they wondered if, perhaps, they had set their sights too high. What, they asked themselves, would the New Year bring?

In January, they knew. Columbia Records liked their demo.

The company wanted to offer them a record contract. All the hard work and dedication had paid off. Now the world, not just Boston, was going to hear from the New Kids on the Block.

The record Maurice Starr and CBS felt was the one to launch the New Kids on a glittering showbusiness career was Be My Girl. The band had been singing it in clubs for months and had got it just right. The New Kids, too, thought it was a perfect choice.

Word spread quickly through Dorchester that another local band had made the breakthrough – another group of kids, white this time, were going to be as famous as New Edition. And, in the weeks leading up to the release of the record in April, excitement mounted.

The New Kids played their work, even more enthusiastically, to friends and anyone else who wanted to listen. Jordan carried a cassette of the record everywhere he went and played it proudly to friends on the school bus. He, like the rest of the band, thought it was a good record that would make their name. They were not cocky, just quietly confident that all the hard work and dedication was going to pay off at last. People in Dorchester thought so, too. Everyone, from David Harris to friendly acquaintances like Joe Gateley, felt that, very soon, the five likeable, ambitious schoolboys would soon be the Most Famous Kids on the Block.

And then the record hit the shops.

And, as summer warmed the streets of Dorchester, the band's hopes of a quick rise to fame began to cool.

Fans in the ghettos liked the record and pushed it into the Top 40 in the black music chart. But it only hovered around the 38 mark, without ever looking like climbing, and failed to have any impact at all on the major record charts. An album, New Kids on the Block, that followed the single, showed signs of making a breakthrough when it was played a lot on local radio stations and by DJs in Boston discos. But, in terms of making the band money, let alone famous, both records and another single later that year – called Didn't I (Blow Your Mind) – were flops.

It was a tough time for the New Kids and they would wrap themselves in the warm friendly atmosphere of the DYC and confide in their pals that they were nervous; that it didn't look good; that maybe all the hard work had been for nothing and they were not going to make it after all.

Friends who had watched them struggle to make something of themselves were supportive. They urged the New Kids not to be downhearted, not to listen to criticism, but to keep faith and to hang on in there.

It was not easy. Whichever way you looked at it, the outlook was grim.

They had done all they could. They had sweated it out, day after day, month after month, learning their craft. They had denied themselves many of the pleasures of youth in search of perfection. They had sung and danced and played their music until they were exhausted.

They had given it their best shot.

And, as 1986 drew to a close, it seemed clear that maybe it wasn't good enough.

The success story continues on page 89

GLITTERING SUCCESS: Jordan, whose voice capitivates millions

FITNESS FANATIC: Danny loves to keep in shape working out in the gym

PUPPY LOVE: Jon wants his Sharpei with him all the time—even backstage

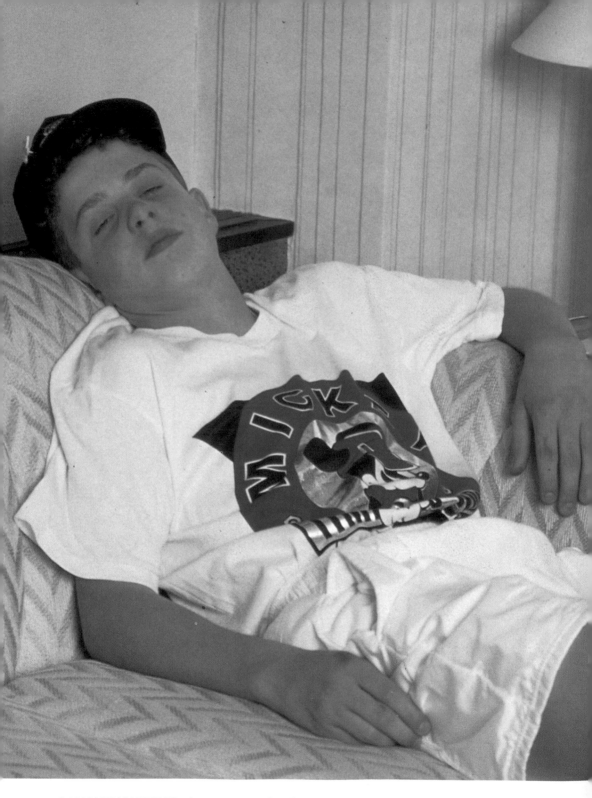
CAUGHT NAPPING: Joey does school work on the road and gets so, so sleepy

STAR-QUALITY: Even as a child, Joey always had a stunning stage presence

SNAPPY DRESSER: Donnie has always taken a great pride in how he looks

STAR-STRUCK: Donnie, the entertainer of Dorchester Park, was born to perform

A KNIGHT EARFUL! Jordan, listening to the screams of young fans

CAP THAT: Joey finds the noise so deafening, he can't hear himself sing

COOL CUSTOMERS: Danny and Joey in unfamiliar headgear on a cold day

IT'S SHOWTIME: Jon's shyness vanishes to get in the mood for the stage

ANGEL EYES: Joey as an altar boy at the wedding of his drama teacher

LITTLE BOY, BIG ROLE: Joey, aged eight, as Oliver and his sister, Carol

ROMANCING THE FANS: Jordan calms the hysteria with a love song

HAPPY FAMILY: Spending so much time together, the New Kids are like brothers

STREET GUYS: Casual New Kids strutt and spin their stuff in a breath-taking dance routine that leaves their fans gasping

WISE GUYS: Smooth New Kids smile and swagger together as Danny slows the tempo for the girls to get their breath back

Danny's home, at
496 Adams Street,
Dorchester

The house at
25 Peverell Street
where Donnie
grew up

ON THE RUN: Danny in a dash for the tape with training mate, Kelly Madden

PRICE OF FAME:
The Knight home at
10 Melville Avenue and
the iron fence the family
was forced to put up

CARING: Jon always has
time for his admirers, no
matter how young

THE JOKERS: Jordan fooling around with boyhood pal, David Harris

THE CHARMER: Jon, with Bertha White, a friend and devoted fan

HELPING OUT: Jon, about to water the plants at school

THE STUDENT: Jon snapped working in the school secretary's office

Joey's house at
20 Orchard Street,
Jamaica Plain

SUMMER DAYS:
Joey, left, aged about
nine, next to
childhood friend, Paul
Callaghan, and two of
Paul's relatives

CLOWNING AROUND: Joey with a friend from the Children's Theatre Group

TAMBOURINE BOY: Joey and Paul Callaghan in a musical mood at Paul's home

STAR ATTRACTION: Joey, aged 10, leading the way in a colourful children's musical

UNFORGOTTEN FRIENDS:
Jonathan Shine and
Paul Callaghan in their
Hangin' Tough tour jackets
and (left) the Lil Peach
where they and Joey shared
their dreams

STAR SPOTTER:
Michelle McCourt at home

PERFECT HARMONY: Joey with sister, Carol

The 160-year-old Footlight Theatre

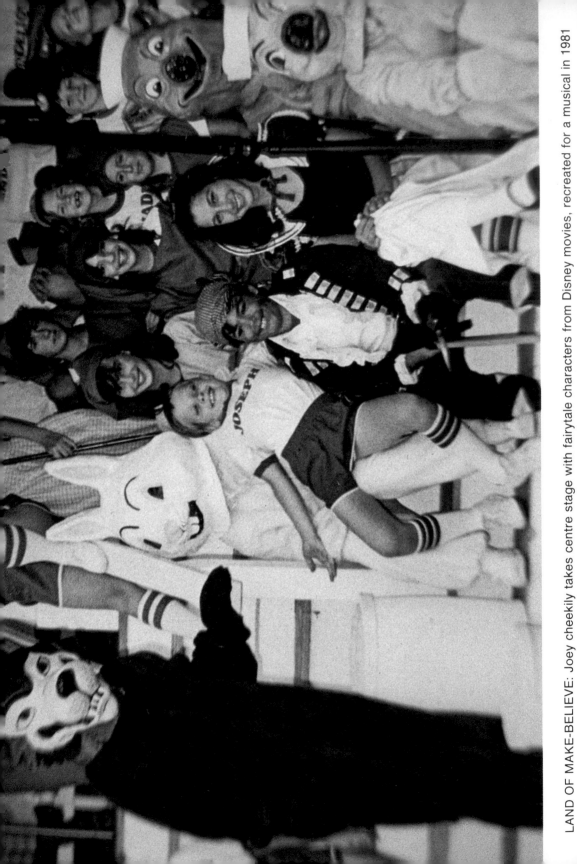

LAND OF MAKE-BELIEVE: Joey cheekily takes centre stage with fairytale characters from Disney movies, recreated for a musical in 1981

PIZZA PALS: Donnie at the popular Hi-Fi Pizza, with Joe Gateley, the man he calls the New Kids' No. 1 Adult Fan, and (left) the restaurant in Dorchester Avenue

HEART AND SOUL:
Passionate music
teacher Rose Holland,
in the classroom where
the New Kids first sang
and (right) the William
Monroe Trotter School
in Roxbury

KIDS STILL ON THE BLOCK: Jamie Kelley (sitting) and Peter Fitzgerald in Dorchester Park

NO REGRETS: Jamie Kelley can't go anywhere without facing the fame he missed, but he insists: "Good luck to the New Kids"

9

Pain of Hangin' Tough

Each of them felt like a champion boxer who had spent months in the gym getting fit for a world title fight, only to lose it. And now, they had a tough decision to make. Should they throw in the towel, and accept that the dream was over? Or should they go back to the gym, and train all over again, even harder this time? And, more important, learn from their mistakes.

The New Kids went back to the gym.

They went back to Roxbury, to the studio that had become a second home, and got down to work again. If they were to win the title, if they were to become champions of the pop world, they had to get on and get it right, not wallow in disappointment.

Donnie was particularly undaunted by the album's flop. As usual, he took a positive attitude; he said the experience was hard to take, but could prove to be *GOOD* for them. It would teach them to deal with failure, so that when they were a success, which they surely would be, they would cherish it more. Far from making them weaker, failure would actually make the New Kids stronger, he stressed.

And so it all started again – with one huge difference this time. In the two years Maurice Starr had been in charge, he had written all the band's material. As a gifted musician, he had dozens of songs in his head and he quickly began writing more for a new album. But he quickly recognised that, in Donnie, Danny and Jordan, he had three youngsters who were bursting with raw song-writing talent, and he encouraged them.

At that time, the boys had written only raps – or, in Jordan's case, short stories for the English High School literary magazine – but they had picked up a lot by watching Maurice on the piano, and what they lacked in experience they made up in enthusiasm. They called themselves The Crickets. And they worked hard to learn their new craft.

Towards the end of the year, the feelings of disappointment that had consumed the band began to fade as a new sharper, tougher album of songs began to take shape. The boxer was changing his style.

If the style and the songs were to be different, something, they all agreed, had to be the same. They had to go back and face those unforgiving black fans in the ghetto clubs and give their new image and music the acid test with live performances, no matter how tough that was going to be. They had to try to prove – again – that a white band performing a black sound was the right stuff for the time. Despite the failure of their album, the principle was still the same: if they could convince the black fans that white kids could sing and dance their music, the white fans would surely follow, and they'd have it made.

The New Kids were still only young teenagers, but, still they felt they could not afford themselves the luxuries of adolescence: games of basketball or baseball or merely hanging out with their friends, doing nothing in particular except enjoying the freedom and lack of pressure that comes with growing up.

As their pals whiled away their evenings in Dorchester Park, the New Kids sweated it out in Roxbury or in the Knights' basement, for up to five hours a night, six days a week. That the boys did not crack under the strain is a credit to their individual characters and, in turn, to the support they received from their families. Not that there wasn't the odd shouting match when the tension got too much; fatigue and impatience, or just plain boredom at going over and over the same routine, made tempers flare. Each time, though, one or more of the group would calm the others down, diffuse the explosive situation and bring them through the troubled patch. Teamwork is about togetherness. And the New Kids, they were going to make sure, would be a hard team to beat.

Slowly, the songs came together. It is not clear which ones came first, but Maurice played all the instruments on every one, except the guitar solo on Cover Girl and I Need You. Certainly the New Kids used their time well in the studio. When they were not actually recording or practising singing or dance routines, they would pick up guitars, trumpets or drums – indeed any instrument – and spend hours trying to learn them. Donnie became hooked on the drums, Jon practised on the wind instruments and Jordan took pleasure teaching Danny some of his keyboard wizardry.

It was a hard, but exciting, time. For the first four months of 1987, they slogged away, perfecting their new songs and dance routines. Maurice Starr was quietly thrilled: he knew what had been wrong before and was certain they had it right this time. The New Kids themselves felt it, too. So they went back into the ghetto to unveil their new look, their tougher image, new sound and slicker stage act. It had been the only way before, and it was the only way now. The New Kids would be nothing if they could not win over Boston's no-nonsense black music fans. The band were nervous, of course. They felt good about their act, but they would not know for sure if it was right until they had performed live.

They need not have worried. The fans loved them, even more than before. And the New Kids went from one ghetto club to another, taking and leaving the stage to mighty applause. The word began to spread around Boston again. The New Kids were back.

Which is why, one day in Spring, Maurice Starr told them: You're ready for the Apollo.

The Apollo Theatre is in the heart of Harlem, the black area of New York. And if the streets there are frighteningly tough, the

91

audience in the theatre is even tougher. The Apollo music fans have no respect for reputation. If performers are lousy on the night, they get a lousy reception. Many artists who have become big stars were booed at the Apollo early in their careers. For the New Kids, that May night when they took on the world's toughest audience was the most nerve-wracking experience of their lives. The prospect made even Franklin Park look tame! Maurice had told them that the Apollo was the ultimate. If they could make it there, he said, they would never be afraid of anywhere again. The huge importance – and the fear – weighed massively on them.

Nervously, the New Kids went out to show the uncompromising crowd in the high temple of R & B music what they could do.

And they brought the house down.

They brought those cynical music lovers to their feet, and left the stage to a deafening standing ovation.

The boxers had trained well. Musically, they were super-fit and ready to go back into the pop ring and take on all-comers for the big prize. The fight began early in 1988 with their new album. The title reflected the band's new "streetwise" image.

It was called: Hangin' Tough.

Aware that there was no room for failure, that they would not get a third chance, Maurice Starr got personally involved in the promotion of Hangin' Tough. Over the first few months of 1988, he badgered radio station disc jockeys into playing the record. They did. But still the New Kids did not have the impact they all felt they would have. Then Maurice and the band's record company released a single from the album. They chose Please Don't Go, Girl, by Joey McIntyre – and it did the trick. It burst into the charts and stormed to No. 10. It was the breakthrough they had been praying for, dreaming of.

America's teenagers loved the adorable little blue-eyed singer, now fourteen, and it gave the band the confidence to talk about going on a nationwide tour. They had spent more than a year learning from their mistakes and now, they wanted to show the whole country what they could do.

At that time, however, the New Kids were not big enough to handle their own tour. They could pack a concert in Boston, of course, but they could not consider trying to do the same in, say, New York or Miami or Los Angeles. Then someone suggested that the New Kids could be the supporting act for a big star. That way hundreds of thousands around the country, who may not have heard of the band, would be able to see them perform live and judge for themselves.

It was a great idea. But there was a snag. Which big star with an appeal to the same young market was making a tour?

Maurice and the band and various helpers behind the scenes put their heads together and came up with Tiffany, a popular teen act who was topping the charts with hits, such as I Saw Him Standing There, All This Time and Could've Been.

The New Kids loved the idea. Tiffany was the perfect choice. Going out on stage before the hottest teenage singer in the country was The Big Break that could transform their lives and make them superstars. The boys started getting excited until Maurice brought them down to earth. They loved Tiffany, he said, but what if Tiffany did not like them? What if she didn't want to give up a prized spot in her stage show to a band who were big in Boston, but who had only one successful single, and a failed album to their name? What if she wanted a very well-known act that would help to guarantee her concerts selling out?

As it turned out, that's precisely what happened. Tiffany was far from convinced that the New Kids would be good for her. Finally, she said she could be tempted, but the New Kids would have to prove they were worthy of a chance. She had been told they were great but she had never seen them herself. If they wanted to appear at her concerts, they would have to fly to wherever she was appearing and perform a personal audition for her. It was a gamble the New Kids were prepared to take.

Which is how, a few days later, Donnie, Danny, Jordan, Jon and Joey came to be standing outside a tiny theatre dressing room in Long Island, New York, waiting to be introduced to the equally tiny pop star.

In the short time they had been on the pop scene the New Kids had had their scary moments. Who could ever forget Franklin

Park when they were booed and pelted with stones? But the audition in front of Tiffany was different. So much depended on it. If she didn't like them, it wouldn't be the end of the world – they would still make records, still have the chance to become famous. But, if she did like them, did want them on her shows, it would be the best thing possible for them. The most important move in their short careers.

The whole experience was nerve-wracking. And, standing outside that tiny dressing room gave them all the jitters. What a strange feeling for five young boys who had performed in front of thousands of fans. At last Tiffany was ready to see them. Slowly, a little shyly, they filed in and were introduced to her and a few members of her entourage. The tension eased. The boys relaxed a little. Tiffany seemed like a nice girl. Maybe the audition wouldn't be so traumatic after all.

The New Kids, it was agreed, had a few minutes to give Tiffany a mini-version of their stage act and sell themselves to her. If she liked them, they were in. If she didn't, thank you and goodbye! The boys took a look around. Doing themselves justice in such a small room, with no stage or special lighting, would not be easy, but they had appeared in many bad venues, and their past experience would have to help them make the best of it.

The boys lined up in front of Tiffany. Someone switched on a portable tape recorder on a table in the corner. Music blared out and the New Kids went into one of the strangest private auditions ever. At times, the cramped conditions made them bump into each other. But they didn't care. They just got on with it, pouring everything they had learned in all those months of practice into the next few minutes, in the most crucial performance of their young lives.

And Tiffany loved them.

They were invited to be the opening act on her forthcoming summer tour. America's teenagers had heard the New Kids on record. Now they were going to see them in the flesh.

The gamble had paid off.

10

Boston goes Bananas

For five young boys who had not travelled much, the coast-to-coast tour was a gruelling experience that sapped their energy and woke them up to the harsh realities of pop stardom the fans don't see. But it was exciting, too, and the confidence of the band grew with every performance. The fans who packed the concerts had come to see Tiffany, of course. But, they seemed to like the band, too. The New Kids would always leave the stage at the end of the first part of the show with huge applause ringing in their ears. Show after show. One town, one city, after another. The applause grew and grew. Gradually, the word was spreading.

And then the Tiffany tour played Boston.

And the city went wild.

A year or so earlier, the New Kids had been licking their wounds after the failure of their first album. Their friends and families, and others who had watched and listened, from a distance, had all wondered whether they had blown it. But the boys had come out fighting, anxious to prove that, for the New Kids on the Block, down did not mean out. Now, they were home again, back among the people who had never lost faith. The boys couldn't wait to prove that those fans were right to support them . . . couldn't wait to show they were a band ready to knock out America.

That day, they ran on to the stage in Boston's Great Woods park to an almighty cheer from fifteen thousand people.

The New Kids' mums – nicknamed The Posse 30 because they have thirty children between them – were in a special enclosure, tingling with excitement like their sons' schoolfriends and everyone else, but trying to keep under control the immense pride they felt at seeing their boys up there.

Proudly, the New Kids showed the people of Boston the new image they had unveiled in other parts of the country. Gone were the rather old-fashioned red sequinned shirts and tight-fitting black trousers. Instead, they were in leather jackets and torn denims – street fashion to fit their "streetwise" image. The crowd loved the new look – and the new sound. They sang and danced and cheered, and the New Kids left the stage to a deafening roar.

They had come home to the people they loved. And it had been a quite breath-taking, triumphant occasion.

It was to be several months before the New Kids would see Boston again. The Tiffany tour rolled on and on, and when they were not supporting her, the band performed in dozens of smaller venues throughout the country.

That year, 1988, was proving to be amazingly successful. Hangin' Tough was entering the Top Ten on the national chart. Please Don't Go, Girl, was still holding its own. And the acclaim the boys had got on the road during the six-week tour promised great things for the future. But it had been a gruelling time that had left the band exhausted. They needed to relax, recharge their batteries, and there was only one place in the world they wanted to get that rest – Dorchester.

The streets certainly didn't have the expensive smell of Los Angeles, the vitality of New York or the luxuriant warmth of Miami. But it was where their families and friends were, where they could switch off and feel comfortable. Dorchester was home and where their hearts were. They had missed it. They couldn't wait to get back.

And, anyway, it would soon be time to put studying before showbiz and go back to school after the summer vacation.

Happily, little had changed. All their friends were still there. Some had got jobs; others were not so lucky. But most were either at school or waiting to go to college. Everyone, youngsters and adults alike, was pleased for the New Kids, and proud of what they had achieved for the town. But they were not ready to treat them as heroes, much less superstars. They were just nice young kids from the neighbourhood who had done well for themselves. And they were treated as such.

It must have been a relief to their friends that the New Kids themselves had not changed, had not let their fame go to their heads.

Jordan's neighbour and long-time pal, David Harris, says: "They were the same guys we had all known for so many years. They hadn't changed or anything. They weren't on big ego trips and didn't want to be treated any differently.

"They would still hang out with the friends they had grown up with. They wouldn't go around shouting, 'Hey, look what we've been doing.'

"Everyone knew about the Tiffany tour and how well the album was doing. We were all pleased for them. Sure, they were proud. But they weren't bragging."

And the Hi-Fi's Joe Gateley is pleased to say: "They would come into the restaurant, but there wouldn't be any great fuss. We would ask how it was going and congratulate them. But they were still the same normal kids and that's how they liked it. Donnie and Jordan would come in for a pizza and a couple of times they brought Joey down, too. Then they would go over to the DYC and meet up with a few old friends.

"Some fans from the neighbourhood would get to know they were in town and track them down for an autograph, but nothing too crazy happened in those days. Even then, nobody saw them as a big deal."

The boys continued to practise, of course, but for the next three months they put their backs into school work, trying to catch up on subjects they may have fallen behind in. By Christmas, the boys were ready for a break from their books – and, temporarily, from their music – and they hung out with all their old pals, happy to be part of the Dorchester way of life they had missed so much.

New Year's Eve. A time for celebration – of thinking back on what had been, and what was to come. The New Kids toasted what had been an astonishing year and wished each other more success in the year to come.

None of them, however – not even Donnie – could have possibly imagined the whirlwind of success and hysteria they were to whip up among millions of America's young girl pop fans over the next twelve months.

It started quickly with an appearance on national television for cerebral palsy, a charity the New Kids had always backed. Then they were asked to perform at New York's famous Madison Square Garden, on behalf of the Sports Youth Fund.

After that, everything, as they say, went crazy. Their funk single, You've Got It (The Right Stuff) stormed to No. 3 in a matter of weeks... and the New Kids On the Block were suddenly the name on everyone's lips and on every TV station. The nation's young pop fans, of course, had known about the band's mass appeal for many months. Now, the whole country knew their faces and their name.

It was five years since that day Gina Marcucci asked her friend, Peter Fitzgerald, if he knew anyone else with talent. Five years since the band had sat in Maurice Starr's studio and listened, somewhat wide-eyed, as he told them they had what it took to become superstars. Five years in which they had worked and sweated with dedication and discipline to get to the top.

Well, now they were there. And if they couldn't really believe it, the newspapers, magazines, radio and TV were always there with the proof.

The dream had, indeed, come true.

11

Life's a Scream

Over the next months, the band were mobbed by near hysterical fans everywhere they went. They got top billing on every national TV pop programme and were asked to appear on top coast-to-coast chat shows. Their faces were on the cover of virtually every teen magazine in the country and even heavyweight news magazines, such as Newsweek, covered their rise to fame.

The band were honoured at the Boston Music Awards with two trophies for The Right Stuff, one for being the most outstanding R&B single and for the video of the song. Then Massachusetts Governor, Michael Dukakis, rewarded the boys for their anti-drug work by naming Monday April 24, 1989, New Kids on the Block Day – one of Boston's highest honours.

Suddenly the young kids from Dorchester were not so much superstars as a pop phenomenon.

The momentum of their success was staggering. And it got stronger. The next single, I'll be Loving You, went to No. 1. The album Hangin' Tough went platinum and was still selling by the thousand. And fan mail was pouring into the boys' homes so fast that their mums had to take charge and set up an official fan club. They arranged a post office box number and made sure fans got a swift reply with a letter, autographed photo, souvenir pin and a membership card. Soon, the volume of mail got too much for them and they had to rent an office, hire full-time staff and get advice from a marketing boss.

* * * * *

It was time for the band to go on tour again to capitalise on their success. Plans were made for them to repeat the successful 1988 Tiffany tour, but everyone soon realised it was ridiculous for the New Kids to support the young singer as before. They were now so big, *SHE* would have to be the warm-up act for *THEM*.

It was a bitter sweet triumph for the New Kids. They knew that without Tiffany they might never had made it so far so quickly. She had generously handed them the spotlight when they were hopeful nobodies and they were grateful. Now, they were faced with taking the spotlight away from her. It wasn't an easy decision, but, no matter how popular she was, Tiffany could not possibly hope to keep the audience's excitement high after their performance. Finally, Tiffany agreed to step down to support act for the 1989 summer tour. Donnie and the rest of the band were not only grateful, but sympathetic to her for having to make the choice.

On August 9 the stage was set once more in Great Woods, Boston, for another Tiffany-New Kids show. This time the New Kids had top billing. Fifteen thousand youngsters cheered Tiffany through her 35-minute performance, but it was clear they were saving their loudest screams for the local boys who had become national superstars.

When the young singer left the stage, the crowd began to pulse with anticipation. The screams and chanting for the New Kids got louder and louder and then the arena erupted in a spine-tingling roar as the boys strutted on to the thumping sound of their song, My Favourite Girl.

It was a thrilling performance and another unforgettable night. Their concerts on that tour were selling out so fast that, after every date, hundreds of heartbroken fans were writing to the promoters, begging for an extra night to be added so they could see their heroes. It was obvious that the New Kids could fill huge stadiums across America, so another, even bigger tour was arranged, with tickets going on sale while the band were still touring with Tiffany. The New Kids had their doubts the tickets would sell. They need not have worried. The stadium concerts sold out almost instantly.

November 9, in Buffalo, New York State. The New Kids opened what was to be a sensational tour – not only financially, but also because it would establish the band as a major pop act. The concert in the town's Memorial Auditorium was not just a run-through of the hits ... it was a glittering spectacular, with pyrotechnics, lasers and giant, inflatable balloons of snowmen and snowcapped cabins. In the past, the New Kids had sung extended versions of seven songs in an hour. Now, they were on stage for one hour, forty minutes and sang twenty songs – with exhausting dance routines to go with them. The hysteria was higher than ever and the band played up to it. Donnie teased the fans by making two sides of the audience compete against one another to prove which was the loudest – with the promise that the winner could take Joey home! In one thrilling moment, Donnie, the master showman, dangled from a gantry plank suspended from the ceiling for an encore of Hangin' Tough. The youngsters of Buffalo loved the New Kids. So did the critics. The show got rave reviews. And the New Kids' popularity climbed even higher.

The New Kids' hi-tech road show swept across America, causing fan mania which newspapers and magazines compared with the Jacksons, the Osmonds and even the Beatles. The band quickly discovered that their followers – known as Blockheads – could be highly imaginative and determined in their efforts to get close to their heroes.

Some have dressed as hotel bedroom maids to try to get on

to the New Kids' floor to tidy up their rooms and grab a souvenir – or actually see the stars. Others have actually climbed into rubbish bins to glimpse the boys leaving hotels by back exits or laid down in front of their limousines. Without fail, all limousine companies in cities where the New Kids are appearing have their telephone lines jammed with calls from fans trying to find out where the cars will be taking the singers.

Security is a major worry. And the New Kids have a heavy-weight back-up team of bodyguards who shadow their every move and check out venues and hotels before the band are allowed in. It is a very serious and frustrating side of their lives, but the boys often make fun of it.

Danny and Joey are the main jokers. The band will be checking into a hotel suite and Danny will suddenly yell at the others not to go into a room before he checks it out. He'll play act and say: "Don't move, guys, there might be snipers in there." Joey will take over and say: "Don't worry, I'm prepared to go in there first and take a bullet for you all." It is all part of the fun they make to keep happy above the strain of being on the road all the time.

As Danny once said: "It's a case of act crazy – or go crazy."

The tour buses are designed to cater for the band's every need. There is a library of books and a vast collection of music and movie videos, and a mini kitchen where they can prepare their own snacks. Sleeping quarters are at the back.

David Harris says the week he spent on tour with the New Kids just before Christmas was "the best week of my life".

"It's kinda crazy, but really exciting," he says. "It's a fast world because you're in a different city nearly every day. But there's no time to get bored. The New Kids get into a town early in the afternoon. They have the rest of the day to relax and enjoy themselves before getting ready for that night's concert. They all like doing different things on their own to switch off, but most of the time they stick together.

"Lately, Danny has got them into training in the gym. Danny is really into fitness and is very health conscious. He likes the others to eat health foods and get all the right vitamins. He lays down the law so much they now call him the Food Cop.

"Danny always checks out the nearest gym and gets the others to go down with him to work out. They all have a go at pushing weights and finish up with a sauna or steam bath. They all enjoy it, especially Danny. He's super fit now."

Jon, on the other hand, prefers to spend time on his own with a Sharpei puppy he bought on tour. However, it was not the breed he dreamed of owning. When he was a boy, he was always talking about getting a Dalmatian, but dropped the idea when the neighbour whose garden he tidied warned they were temperamental and hard to handle.

But, in a way, that woman helped Jon realise his boyhood dream. She's an artist and made two life-size, Dalmatian models in papier-mache which Jon bought for his bedroom.

On tour the real-life dog is Jon's best friend. David Harris says: "Jon loves that Sharpei and has it around him all the time. The dog sits on his lap in the tour bus, sleeps in his hotel room and even goes back-stage.

"The dog is a great comfort for Jon. He likes to take things nice and slow and not get worked up about their shows. On the bus, he'll sit staring out the window for hours just looking at the scenery. He is fascinated at how the landscape changes from state to state.

"Jordan is very different. He'll watch videos, especially music ones. He'll keep replaying tapes of Bobby Brown and Michael Jackson – even in slow motion – to learn the steps to their dance routines. He's always trying to learn something new. Even when he's lying down, trying to have a nap, he'll hum a tune to himself. If he's not watching tapes, he'll practise on an instrument. He is always trying to improve himself.

"Donnie is the clown on the road. He's a real joker and has so much energy. He's really wild and keeps everyone alive and entertained if they're feeling a bit low. If Donnie is not talking to one of the band, he is up front talking with the bus driver or somebody else.

"Joey is fairly quiet a lot of the time. He spends most of the time trying to catch up on his sleep."

Joey is still a pupil at Boston's $2,000-a-year Catholic Memorial High School, but has been on the road so long he has attended classes only two or three times a year since he was fourteen.

He keeps up with lessons from his travelling tutor, Mark O'Dowd, nicknamed Freud by the band because he "knows everything". "Freud" goes to see Joey's headmaster, Anthony Portilo, every month to report on the young star's academic progress – and the head is never disappointed. Joey is an A-grade student and he plans to graduate with the rest of his classmates next year. Already, the school is thinking of security arrangements because thousands of fans will probably want to be at the award ceremony. Joey is so proud of the school, he has performed on stage and appeared on television in a sweat shirt bearing its name.

The band still love sport and never miss the chance to play basketball whenever their schedule allows.

David Harris says: "If they go to a gym or YMCA, it has to be closed off so that they don't get mobbed or put off by having a big crowd watching them. In Los Angeles, we played around on the beach, virtually unnoticed, which the boys loved. But they are great towards their fans. If one does ask for an autograph or for a picture with them, they always try to do it. I've never known them to refuse.

"If any of the boys want to go somewhere, a bodyguard usually goes with them. But, in Chicago, one night, I sneaked out with Donnie and Jordan and went to the movies. We got away with it – no one recognised them."

Before each show, the New Kids and Maurice Starr go through a two-minute ritual no one would ever dare interrupt. They huddle up in a tight circle in the dressing room, or behind the stage, and pray. They close their eyes and hold each other's hands and one of the boys, or Maurice, says a prayer to thank God for their musical talent, and to bless each other and their families and the ones they love.

"It's something they've been doing for years," says David

Harris. "It was either Donnie's or Maurice's idea and it began when they played their first gig at the Lee High School.

"It takes a lot of concentration to perform in front of thousands of people and that precious time just before they go on is when they bring all their thoughts together and prepare themselves. They take turns to say the prayer and it is interesting to watch.

"Years ago, they set a bond between them – rather like an oath – saying they were a group and would not split up. The praying helps keep that bond solid.

"Maurice is nearly always backstage, encouraging the band and making sure they are happy with everything. If anything is not quite right, he tries to get it changed. Before they go on stage, each one of the boys starts getting psyched up. They're not actually nervous, more excited, and anxious to get going. Seconds before they run out, they slap each other's hands as a final sign for good luck. You can see on their faces how much they love it. I'm lucky to have seen them come from playing in a junk yard in Dorchester to huge arenas, with an orchestra backing them. It's an unbelievable experience.

"Because I'm a close friend, I watch the boys from the front. They like to play around a bit and make jokes. I have stood right at the front and made faces at them just to try to make them laugh. But they have become true professionals and it's rare for them to make mistakes. If they do, they're covered up instantly. They care so much about putting on a good show.

"A few times, they let me warm up the audience for them. Once, I went out in front of 17,000 fans and got them screaming for the New Kids. Watching the boys perform while growing up rubbed off on me and I can rap pretty good. So, on the stage, I was saying things like: 'Put your hands in the air, wave 'em like you just don't care. This is the regular rock – with New Kids on the Block. Somebody yell, Oh, Yeah!' and the audience would all start shouting back at me. That's a feeling I'll never forget, an unbelievable experience. It was great to get the chance.

"They're on stage for around an hour and 45 minutes and have a show virtually every night. When I was with them, they had had only one day off in three months. At times they have travelled through three or four states in the space of a day for some promotion work.

"When they were starting out they would come off stage totally exhausted, but they are fitter now and are usually so high they don't think about being tired. Their bodies are now so used to performing that they could go on through the night if they had to. After a show they might go to a nightclub or a party and dance some more, but most times they go back to the hotel and sleep. They're usually in bed by one or two in the morning and up at nine to move on to another city. In the week I was on tour, we went to Chicago, Iowa City, Kansas City and Los Angeles.

"It is strict for them on tour and no girls are allowed in the hotels. They have a single room each, always on the same floor. Sometimes, after a show, they will all go into one room and watch TV and a movie together.

"The boys have a honey and lemon drink to soothe the strain on their voices and they eat a lot of protein to keep them strong. They're all very healthy.

"You'd expect a group of boys who spend so much time together would argue a lot. But the New Kids don't. They go to the same places and meet the same people, but they are all so happy together. When I was on tour with them, I didn't once see them fall out badly over anything. I'm not saying they agree on everything – that would be stupid. But if one of them has a different point of view – like the way to do a dance routine or a song – they just talk it through until they come up with something everyone is happy with. It's important to them to talk things through, even personal problems. The atmosphere is very much like a big family. The boys are like brothers.

"When I travelled with them, they treated me just the same as they do when we're back home. They still joke around with me and have a laugh. I felt very relaxed hanging out with them. I didn't know Danny too well before I joined them, but I got the chance to talk with him and we got on well. He's very intelligent, and knows what he wants to do with his life. He was always the one who wanted to practise the hardest in the early days. He's a hard worker and that shows when they are on tour.

"Jon is nearly always the first up in the mornings, because the puppy wakes him so early. Jordan and Joey are the last. Everyone normally hits the road without having breakfast, but first they have to plan a smooth escape route through the mass of fans waiting outside. Often, the entourage will switch exits at the last minute, to make sure there isn't a massive crush when the boys finally come out. I found the crowd hysteria amazing. When you go on tour you get to realise the extent of their fame, just how much the boys are loved."

12

New Kings on the Block

The New Kids get very homesick and keep in constant touch with friends and family by telephone. Jon and Jordan will call their mum nearly every time they reach a new town – and the calls can last an hour.

All the band are fiercely proud of their Boston roots and have tried hard not to forget the people who helped and encouraged them when they were younger and just boys from the neighbourhood.

On one visit back home, they called in to see their former music teacher, Rose Holland. They went to the Trotter school in Roxbury to thank her personally for giving them the "soul" which had shaped their success.

"I was on my own in the classroom, going through some music, when they just walked through the door," Rose says. "All four of them were there and they had brought little Joey McIntyre, too. I couldn't believe what I was seeing.

"I don't buy popular records and, at that time, I didn't know the extent of their fame. But I found it all very exciting. They said they had come to thank me for pushing them so hard in the chorus. They seemed to feel I was the one responsible for getting them interested in music and encouraging them to get involved with it. They said I had given them a feeling for music. I felt so proud.

"Donnie – it had to be Donnie – was the spokesman. He said: 'Miss Holland, all this started with you.' I was amazed. I said

'Really?' and then Jon, Jordan and Danny grinned and said: 'Yeah, that's right. You're the one.' Then Donnie laughed and said: 'I know you don't believe I'm in this, Miss Holland – I know you didn't think I would do anything in music.' That was because he had been so uninterested and naughty during lessons when he was a little boy.

"I was tongue-tied while I was listening to them say those things. I just kept saying 'I can't believe this . . . I can't believe it.'

"They were all standing there in a line, so grown up and so handsome. Then I asked them if they could sing something there and then for me. It would have been wonderful for me, but they had someone with them from their management who, for some reason, told them it wasn't allowed. It was something to do with their contract.

"I didn't really understand. The room was so small, I don't think it would have done any harm. But it never happened. I was so disappointed and upset. I would have loved to have heard the boys sing together again and I got the impression they would have loved to sing for me, too. I wanted so much for them to stay longer and talk, and was sad to see them go.

"After that visit, some of my pupils brought in the New Kids' records, Hangin' Tough and The Right Stuff, for me. I was pleasantly surprised. I played them in the classroom and thought, Gee – what a lovely harmony. They're really good. They have put in an amazing amount of hard work and Maurice Starr has groomed them brilliantly.

"But I feel the Trotter school and I can take some credit for all their energy, and the fact that they became such good friends and stayed together. It's all about team work. We think of the school as a team and a family where each person has their worth and it is what is inside that really counts.

"So many of my pupils are New Kids' fans and they're always asking me about them. They ask what they were like and what they got up to when they were younger. I say 'They were just like you all and four of them used to sit just where you are now and you all could be like them if you're prepared to work for it.'

"There's a book in which Donnie signed his name when he was a pupil here, and all my kids queue up to look at it time after time. We like to put up newspaper stories about the boys on the notice board so the children can keep up to date with them. I also keep a video tape of interviews with them. When I put that on, I love to sit back and watch my pupils' faces light up. I would love the boys to come back and visit again and meet some the children this time. But I suppose it would have to be done secretly to avoid the fuss.

"Lately, my kids have asked me if they can learn one of the New Kids' songs – This One's For The Children – and I've promised to get the music to do it for them. So, the music of the boys will live on at the Trotter school."

Keeping in touch has not been easy and the New Kids have had to pay a price for fame – their privacy. As their popularity has risen, so their private lives have become complicated. Now, it is almost impossible for them to go anywhere without drawing a crowd or being mobbed. It has got so bad that they have sometimes had to go round wearing dark glasses, with baseball caps pulled low over their faces.

Their homes are constantly besieged by fans. Some have been caught crawling through gardens or climbing trees with binoculars. Others wait for rubbish bins to be put out, so that they can sift through for souvenirs. Chunks of lawn have been dug up and taken away. Even leaves from trees have become prized possessions for devoted Blockheads.

The Knight family got so fed up with fans walking across their lawn that they erected a six-foot iron fence with electric gates at the front of the house. The fans' intrusion affects Jon mainly because he likes to spend time in the garden. Now, he is more likely to retire to his bedroom where he keeps exotic fish in a large tank.

The family's close friend, Father Oakes, has seen the effect of fame at first hand and, last October, was able to bring some normality into Jon's life.

He says: "The band had two or three days off and Jon said he really wanted to get away. He couldn't stay at home because there were always girls with their noses pressed against the front windows. So I took him and his mother to my house at the top of a mountain in Maine, a couple of hundred miles from Dorchester. It was wonderful. Jon was able to go into a store and buy a can of coke and eat in restaurants without being bothered. We walked through the little village and Jon said he hadn't been able to do that for a whole year. For once, he was able to be a normal twenty-year-old! Not once in three days did anyone come up to him and say: 'Hey, aren't you . . .?'

"We went to a friend's house for a drink. They had two daughters – aged four and six – and I suggested taking a New Kids' poster, so the girls would know who they had met. I went in and said: 'Look who I have brought to see you,' thinking they would get all excited.

"But they were too young and had never heard of the New Kids on the Block. I gave them a video to watch while we were there and afterwards they came up to Jon and gawped at him. No doubt, later in their lives they'll regret that they weren't old enough to appreciate the experience.

"When the New Kids got back from their U.S. tour, on Christmas Eve they were exhausted. Jon slept for 24 hours and didn't know if it was Christmas or Easter. They had their Christmas hits in the charts and Jon said how peculiar it was because they had been singing the songs since October – and, no doubt, would be singing them well into January! He said it was so unlike the traditional Christmas celebrations which only go on for twelve days. For him and the New Kids, Christmas went on and on. He admitted he missed not being at home to enjoy the normal Christmas build-up.

"But, despite all those sort of feelings, Jon and Jordan are extremely grateful for their rise to fame. They certainly don't take it for granted. One of them – I forget who – told me that, if they do begin to get irritated at the fan hysteria, they have to remember it is because of the fans that they are where they are today, and they snap out of it."

Before the fence was put up, some fans did go too far and

really upset Jon. He had planted a special tree in his front garden as a Mothers' Day gift and the girls unwittingly destroyed it in the rush to crowd round him.

"He was very, very sad about that," said Father Oakes. "He didn't think anyone knew he was there. But the fans seem to know before anyone else when the boys are home and congregate outside their home for hours on end. One day, the house was besieged by scores of young girls when Jon and Jordan were about to leave for the airport. They waited for ages and finally drove out, hiding in the boot of their brother David's car!

"It really upsets Jon if he has to ignore people because he is the type of boy who has always had time for everyone. Last Christmas, for example, my mother, who is 90, was on a visit from England and the Knight family had popped into the church for a chat. I had to go out for a while and, when I came back, I found her and Jon engrossed in conversation, like long-lost friends. He was telling her all about his experiences as a celebrity and promising to visit her in England when the band tours there. Jon's the sort of boy who won't forget."

Despite the fans' adulation, the band try to stay in touch with the simple life of Dorchester they love so much and try really hard to keep contact with old school friends.

The Hi-Fi pizza shop and the Lil Peach in Jamaica Plain have become shrines to the New Kids because the fans know they still go there. Some fans travel from all parts of America, just to hang around there in the hope of seeing one of their heroes.

One girl, Deirdre MacDonagh, who is fourteen, is driven to Dorchester every Saturday by her mother from their home in New Hampshire . . . eighty miles away! Deirdre hangs around the Hi-Fi all day until she is picked up in the evening. She feels it has been worth it, because, once, she met Danny, Joey and, her favourite, Donnie.

A collage of photographs of the band takes pride of place in the restaurant, next to the juke box which is always playing New Kids' hits. When Donnie or one of the others go there to eat they have to sit in the back while the owners do their best to keep fans away. But once the boys leave, the fans swoop on the sacred table hoping to grab a left-over pizza crust, a cup, or even a paper plate.

Joe Gateley, who remembers the days when the band could barely afford one slice of pizza, is pleased they still go there – even though they could buy their own shop. He says: "Only a month ago, I was leaning over a bench wiping down one of the tables when Donnie came up, slapped me on the back of the head, and said: 'Hey, come on, I've been waiting.' You know, giving me a hard time. But he was joking around – it was all in fun. He was letting me know he was still the same cheeky Donnie and that nothing had changed.

"He could only spare a couple of minutes because he was in a hurry to get to the studio. But he said: 'I can't go by without coming in because I love this place. I was in Texas and all I could think of was Hi-Fi pizza. They're the best in America and I miss them.' It was a nice thing to say. The pizzas aren't really that different, but Dorchester is Donnie's home town and this is where he used to hang out. That kind of thing is important to someone like Donnie. He's been coming here for as long as I can remember. He used to spend hours over one piece of pizza."

Joe believes that fame has changed people's attitude towards the band more than it has changed the boys themselves. "They act as if everything's the same, but I'm sure they must notice a difference in the way we treat them," he says. "We treat them like stars. Certainly I do. I'm slightly in awe of them because of what they have accomplished. Donnie calls me his Number One Adult Fan, which I like. I'm nuts over them."

So are Joe's own kids, Jennifer, fourteen, Gillian, eleven, and Jake, five. They have more than 200 pictures of the band on their walls.

One day Jordan came into the Hi-Fi with some friends and ordered some sandwiches. Dozens of fans were hanging around outside, so he said he was going to the DYC a few doors along and would come back for the sandwiches later. Joe offered to take them. Ten minutes or so later he was walking back to the restaurant after giving Jordan the sandwiches, when a thought struck him.

"I realised suddenly that Jordan had paid me with money out of his own pocket," Joe said. "I had dollar bills he had *actually touched*. So I paid for the sandwiches out of my own money and kept his. When I got home I gave Jordan's money to my kids and they were so thrilled they pinned the bills on their walls. They're so proud and tell all their friends. It's amazing the effect the New Kids have on you.

"They treat everyone really well and don't forget their friends. When they played Boston last year I couldn't get tickets – until the day of the concert when Donnie breezed into the shop with Danny.

"Both of them chatted to me for a while, then left saying: 'See ya tonight after the show.' When I told them I couldn't get tickets, Donnie told me not to worry – tickets for the whole family would be waiting at the box office. I couldn't wait to tell my kids. I was more excited than them.

"Donnie gave us wonderful seats in the second row with all their families around us. It was an unbelievable, magical night, and, as I watched Donnie on stage, I was angry with myself for thinking so badly of him all those years ago.

"I should be the one who treats him like someone because of what he has done, but he treats *me* like I'm somebody. He's certainly taught me a lesson – that you should never judge people by the way they look."

Many people in Jamaica Plain thought Joey McIntyre would change under the weight of all the female hysteria. But, like his pals from Dorchester, he has remained the same likeable guy whose feet are firmly on the ground. He hasn't forgotten his two tearaway pals, Jonathan Shine and Paul Callaghan. He not only gave them Hangin' Tough tour jackets, but also a surprise Christmas present – $1,000 each.

Jonathan said: "He's still the same old Cloey we have known all these years. But, sadly, his success has changed what he can do in his life. He likes to hang out at the Lil Peach like in the old days, but the fans soon get to know, so we have to do other things – like go to the movies or play basketball. He's always telling me how homesick he gets on tour. He really enjoys himself, but misses the simple things so much.

"He has a concert every night, sleeps during the day, and then he's up again to go on stage. He gets so tired. He rings up all the time – sometimes from a limo when he is being driven around. Every five months or so, he comes home for about three weeks, but he always wants to stay longer. He's just slipping back into the routine around here when it's time to go back on the road.

"Cloey loved the fame at first, but now he hates it. He rarely gets much peace. I've gone to restaurants with him, just for a hamburger, and half way through the meal the fans come in and ask him all kinds of questions. And all that is in the middle of a meal on his nights off. It's inhuman and I'd hate it. But Cloey says it is a small price to pay for the success they're having and he tries to take it all in his stride."

Paul Callaghan's sister, Paula, feels that Joey is still the same cute kid who grew up in the neighbourhood. "Whenever he comes over for dinner, he still clears the table and helps with the dishes," she said. "I'm sure the fans who see him as a big star wouldn't expect him to be doing that sort of thing."

Both Jon and Jordan keep in touch with friends, including David Harris and Bertha White. Bertha said: "One night just before Christmas I went out for a meal with Jon and some school friends and found him to be the same caring, generous person I knew before. Another time, Jon took a couple of friends and I out in his jeep. I expected him to drive slowly and carefully, but he started swerving all over the road to scare everyone. It was a long, straight road with no other cars around, so we were all laughing. He may have a serious side, but he likes to have fun."

David Harris says his friendship with Jordan has not changed either. "He's always calling me while on tour, and when he gets back he rings straight away. We've known each other so long that if either of us had a problem we would be there for each other. The same goes for our families. In fact, my father has always considered Jordan another son. And, often, when we're all together, Jordan will call him Dad."

All the New Kids are anxious to use their fame and influence by speaking out against drugs and racism, and encouraging youngsters to work hard at school. The band has performed at many anti-drug concerts and one of their fan phones lines carries the message: "Say No to drugs."

Donnie is particularly vocal against drugs because it is a sad problem that has affected some of his family. One brother, Jimbo, was jailed for three years on cocaine charges and Donnie supported him strongly. He visited him regularly and took him expensive presents – including gold chains – to keep him cheerful. Donnie even interrupted a TV interview to send his good wishes to Jimbo – not mentioning he was in jail, of course.

Jimbo was released from a Boston prison in February and Donnie has encouraged him to do community work, instead of drifting back into crime. An inmate who served time with Jimbo said:

"Donnie is a very loyal brother and helped Jimbo get through his sentence. He kept in touch constantly and encouraged Jimbo to go straight and get his life sorted out when he was released.

"Jimbo is very proud of Donnie and used to get a thrill out of seeing him on TV and reading about him in the newspapers. It used to help him get through the tough time he had inside. When Donnie visited, he always lifted Jimbo's morale."

The New Kids are determined to put something positive back into Dorchester and there is talk of them donating money to build a new youth centre in the town.

Donnie is also producing an album for the Northside Boys, an up-and-coming young Dorchester band. And he and Danny have gone back to the Daniel Marr Boys and Girls Club, to play basketball with the youngsters and talk against drugs. Once, Donnie went out of his way to have his photo taken with a fan with a serious heart condition, who had travelled five hours from Connecticut.

Bob Scannell, who runs the club, feels the boys are good role models for the youngsters. He says: "Donnie's mother showed me some of the fan letters. Nearly all said things like: 'I will never take drugs or drink, because you think it's bad and you might not like me.' Children all over the country are getting the message that drugs are bad because of what the band has said."

At the DYC, Emmett Folgert said: "The New Kids are very caring towards the younger members here. They hug and play with them and take them out for pizzas. When one young boy saw Donnie wearing sun glasses he said they would look dope – slang for good – with his jacket. Donnie took the glasses off and gave them to him and the boy gave him something in return. The band used to trade things all the time when they were kids and they still do it.

"They're very proud of Dorchester and Boston and always talk about the city in interviews. In the past, Boston has been famous for its criminals and not much else. Many think Dorchester youngsters are losers. But the New Kids are proving that we have lots of talent here and a lot of positive things to offer. The New Kids could easily have turned their backs on such a poor neighbourhood and said: 'Right, I'm outta here.' But they love to come home."

In January, the boys from Boston were honoured with two top awards at the prestigious American Music Awards in Los Angeles. Hangin' Tough was voted the best album of 1989 and the New Kids the top pop-rock band. It was a fitting tribute to a band which has outsold some of the most established stars in the world. And, like all rags-to-riches stories, the statistics behind the hysteria are mind-boggling.

In March 1990, the Hangin' Tough album had sold 7.6 million copies in America. The New Kids' other album – the re-released

New Kids on the Block – 2.3 million and their third album, Merry, Merry Christmas, more than 2 million.

Their seven singles in America also had phenomenal success. In 1988, Please Don't Go, Girl reached No. 10. Then, last year, two records went to No. 1 – I'll Be Loving You (Forever), and Hangin' Tough. Cover Girl got to No. 2, You've Got It (The Right Stuff) reached No. 3, while Didn't I (Blow Your Mind) got to No. 8. The band's latest single, This One's For The Children, was still climbing the charts.

The band has also had No. 1 hits in Canada, Australia, and Japan. The Right Stuff and Hangin' Tough went to the top in the British charts, with the album selling 600,000. And on March 18th, I'll Be Loving You (Forever), soared to No. 5 after just two weeks.

The New Kids' fan club receives around 30,000 letters every day and about 100,000 calls a week are made to a series of telephone hotlines, generating at least $200,000 a week.

Early this year, the band sealed a $3 million deal for television commercials for Coca Cola, now showing in the States. A weekly cartoon series and a full-length feature film are also on the cards.

After their ten-date sell-out tour of Britain, the New Kids return to America to begin yet another tour. The band have also launched New Kids' dolls, complete with plastic stage and microphones, and have already laid the tracks for their fourth album, to be released this summer.

Donnie, Danny, Jon, Jordan and Joey deserve their success, their acclaim and, yes, their money. They knew what they wanted and they went for it. They worked when they could have played. They sweated it out when it would have been easy to quit.

They went off as kids in search of a dream.

And they came back as stars . . . the New Kings on the Block.

The fairytale that began under those towering trees in Dorchester Park, has, indeed, come true.

THE END

(But the success story continues)

Where are the Friends now?

Jamie Kelley, nearly nineteen now, is trying to get his life together after drifting from one poorly-paid job to another. He has gone back to school to study for his High School Diploma and hopes to get the qualifications to become an environmental engineer.

After he was booted out of Nynuk in 1985, Jamie went downhill fast in his search for a good time. He dropped out of school without passing any exams and took the first job he could find – shovelling mud and carrying plants for a landscape gardener.

As his friends in the band became the New Kids on the Block and capitalised on their talent, Jamie went from one dead end job to another and finally ended up sweeping Dorchester's streets.

"Oh, yes, I took the evil road all right – and I went downhill fast," he admits. "You can't get much lower than a roadsweeper, working in all weathers for a lousy seven dollars an hour, can you? I got so depressed, I'd pick up my wages at the end of the week and head for the nearest bar to forget what a mess I'd made of things. I would be smashed all weekend and, by Sunday night, I'd have blown all my money.

"I don't feel bitter about the New Kids. It would be crazy to say I wouldn't want their lifestyle, but I'm not jealous. It's something I never had. I only came close to it.

"The guys worked hard and deserve everything they've got. When I was with them, I just wanted cash in my hand to have a good, easy time. I wasn't prepared, like them, to live on the promise of a dream that *might* come true in a few years.

"They took the good road and have fame and fortune. I took the bad road and ended up with nothing. But I've got off that road now and am working hard in school to make something of my life. I'm still only nineteen, after all."

Peter Fitzgerald, a highly-intelligent, charming twenty-year-old, laughs when you ask him if he's jealous that he isn't a New Kid on the Block with a million in the bank.

"Why should I be?" he asks. "I didn't miss the chance of

119

anything. Okay, I was part of the start, but all the fame happened after I left. Far from being jealous, I'm pleased for the guys – particularly Donnie. He always wanted to be a big star. And, honestly, I always thought he was destined for something like that.

"I've only seen him once since he became a superstar. We bumped into each other at the shopping mall in Dorchester and talked for a few minutes. He was fine, very friendly."

As a teenager, Peter spent part of his summer vacation helping in a camp for mentally-handicapped children in a little New Hampshire town. After High School, where he graduated with lots of qualifications, including carpentry and building technology, he worked full-time with special needs people in Dorchester for a year. Now, he is in his first year at Dorchester's Massachussetts University, studying liberal arts.

Jonathan Shine is still at school and plans to start training to be a cordon bleu chef next year.

He says: "I'm pleased and very proud of Joey. I would love to be a singer with all the fame he has, but I would also love to be a chef and buy my own restaurant. I will – one day. I know I came close to getting the job with the New Kids, but I don't feel bitter about it. I'm pleased for Joey that he is all set and having a great time. But I also see how tired he is on the road. Everyone thinks he just sings for a living but I know his life is tough and he has to work hard."

David Harris still lives around the corner from the Knight home in Melville Avenue and is as close as ever with Jordan. David has started up his own rapping band with the boys' adopted brother, Chris, and they have called themselves The Goat Brothers, a name invented by Donnie and Jordan.

To help the band on their way, Maurice Starr has given them a four-track music machine – the same one he used to record the New Kids in Roxbury!